P9-CLC-760

The Pullman Case

LANDMARK LAW CASES

AMERICAN SOCIETY

Peter Charles Hoffer
N. E. H. Hull
Series Editors

Other titles in the series:

Peter Charles Hoffer
The Salem Witchcraft Trials:
A Legal History

Harold M. Hyman
The Reconstruction Justice of Salmon P. Chase:
In Re Turner *and* Texas v. White

John W. Johnson
The Struggle for Student Rights:
Tinker v. Des Moines *and the 1960s*

Paul Kens
Lochner v. New York:
Economic Regulation on Trial

Philippa Strum
When the Nazis Came to Skokie:
Freedom for Speech We Hate

Melvin I. Urofsky
Affirmative Action on Trial:
Sex Discrimination in Johnson v. Santa Clara

DAVID RAY PAPKE

The Pullman Case

The Clash of Labor and Capital

in Industrial America

UNIVERSITY PRESS OF KANSAS

Published by the University Press of Kansas (Lawrence, Kansas 66049), which was
organized by the Kansas Board of Regents and is operated and funded by Emporia State
University, Fort Hays State University, Kansas State University, Pittsburg State
University, the University of Kansas, and Wichita State University.

Library of Congress Cataloging-in-Publication Data

Papke, David Ray, 1947–

The Pullman case : the clash of labor and capital in industrial

America / David Ray Papke.

p.   cm. — (Landmark law cases & American society)

Includes bibliographical references and index.

ISBN 0-7006-0953-9 (cloth : alk. paper). — ISBN 0-7006-0954-7

(pbk. : alk. paper)

1. Debs, Eugene V. (Eugene Victor), 1855–1926.—Trials,
litigation, etc. 2. Trials (Conspiracy)—Illinois. 3. Strikes and
lookouts—Railroads—Law and legislation—United States—History.
4. Chicago Strike, 1894. [1. Pullman, George Mortimer, 1831–1897.]

I. Title. II. Series.

KF223.D435P37   1999

344.7301'892385—dc21   98-50880

British Library Cataloguing in Publication Data is available.

Printed in the United States of America

10 9 8 7 6 5 4 3 2 1

The paper used in this publication meets the minimum requirements of the American
National Standard for Permanence of Paper for Printed Library Materials Z39.48-1984.

FOR JOHN RAYMOND PAPKE, MY SON

CONTENTS

Industrial workers have never been a majority of this country's labor force, but their struggle for recognition and autonomy has attracted the attention of many skilled scholars. With this book on Eugene V. Debs and the Pullman strike, David Ray Papke joins the list. The history of the labor union movement is filled with dramatic and tragic incidents and heroic as well as mean-spirited actors, and the episode herein recounted is emblematic of the forces and the players in the larger story. For however just the cause of the union organizers and their followers may have been, they faced an uphill battle against better financed and less "threatening" corporate leaders, managerial agents and nonunion employees. These groups' interests—as employers and consumers—led them to fundamentally misperceive the needs and reject the demands of their unionized workforce. Add to this antipathy for the working class the idea that laborers at any individual factory or workplace greatly outnumbered management. It is understandable that as a result, employers feared combinations of workers.

The legal side of this story is just as fascinating, and Papke tells a complex tale of courts, judges, and injunctions. In fact, labor unions had only recently become lawful, when Eugene V. Debs brought his American Railway Union into the fray on the side of the striking Pullman Railway Car factory workers. What had begun as a combat between a paternalistic and authoritarian owner and "his" workers soon escalated into a strike that paralyzed rail traffic in much of the Midwest. The state of Illinois and the federal government entered the fray as the union disrupted rail traffic and the politicians fussed. Soon federal troops and special police arrived to protect the strikebreakers the railowners had brought in from all over the country.

The courts might not have been the best place to resolve this dispute, but to the courts rushed lawyers for the affected companies, seeking injunctive relief. Injunctions were one of the tools that the old English chancellor used against those who refused to act in good faith during a court proceeding. In America, until the 1890s injunctions had been a weapon that homeowners, small farmers, and city folk used against nuisances like smelly factories and polluting mills. Increasingly thereafter they became the tool of capital against labor, for by enjoining strikers, courts gave companies time to hire nonunion workers. In the Pullman case, friendly judges allowed the railway managers to deploy the injunction against Debs and his comrades, who violated the court orders at peril of criminal contempt citations and jail time.

Behind the Pullman case lay a conflict of economic ideologies at a watershed time in our nation's history. The old theory of free labor assumed that the employee and the employer could bargain on equal terms. In fact, giant corporations like the railroads had far greater bargaining power than any individual—for labor was cheap in a nation filling rapidly with immigrants from all over the world. Legislatures (including Illinois's) were not unfriendly to the concerns of labor, often passing legislation to improve workplace safety, limit hours, and curb child labor, but the federal government, in particular the federal courts, did not allow all of these measures to stand. The new laws faced a stern test against prevailing economic orthodoxies. Among these traditional premises, one, "liberty of contract," became a watchword for conservative jurists and antiunion judges and a vital fiction for companies struggling to control labor costs in a period of cutthroat competition.

Papke's book captures the passions of that turbulent age, when everyone took sides. His word portraits of the leadership of both sides, his clear and straightforward explanations of the legal maneuvers and arguments, and his moving account of the later lives of the participants brings us much closer to an age that laid the groundwork for our own.

The notions and terms we use to understand social conflict have changed dramatically from those employed in the late nineteenth century. With the sale of services exceeding that of goods and a world economy taken for granted, Americans rarely reflect on the processes and traumas of "industrialization." With union memberships declining and corporate ownership dispersed, we seldom perceive a struggle between "capital" and "labor." At the end of the nineteenth century, however, these were precisely the notions and terms that dominated discourse. The struggle between capital and labor in the industrial sector seemed not only significant in and of itself but also crucial to the future of the Republic.

When Americans of that era reflected on industrialization, they of course contemplated the increased production of goods by machine rather than by hand and the shift of workers from agriculture to manufacturing. But "industrialization" was much more than that. It included as well the construction of immense, carefully organized factories and industrial plants and the expanded use of new inventions and technologies in those factories and plants. Industrialists accumulated capital in unprecedented amounts in order to build and expand, and industrial workers found their tasks increasingly routinized, specialized, and dictated by the clock. They now worked for daily and hourly wages, and they frequently relocated in order to achieve not better jobs but higher wages. Manufactured goods themselves were sold in national rather than local markets, and expanded communication and transportation systems facilitated market development.

As late as the 1890s parts of the country still had few factories, and farmers continued to outnumber industrial workers in absolute numbers. But "industrialization" was clearly the cutting edge of socioeconomic development. The United States had become the most productive industrial nation in the world. Many Americans thought that because of industrialization a whole new world was dawning. Some were inspired by the changes, while others were fretful and frightened.

A large part of the fear derived not from just the headlong race into an unknown future but rather from the severe tension between opposing forces in the industrial sector: "capital" and "labor." Earlier in the century few would have perceived or spoken of this opposition. Farmers had sometimes taken issue with urban artisans and vice versa. More commonly, both farmers and artisans complained not about "capital" but rather about financiers, bankers, speculators, and others who seemed engaged in a type of dishonest labor. But in the decades immediately following the Civil War, "capital" and "labor" seemed to many the most pronounced poles of opposition.

Both terms have interesting and complicated histories. The economic use of the term "capital" had appeared in English language usage in the seventeenth century and involved a shortening of the phrase "capital stock": a material holding or monetary fund. The term, even in its economic sense, also carried the earlier and still common notions of "head" or "chief." "Labor," by contrast, had come in the eighteenth century to stand for that element of production that in combination with capital and raw materials led to produced or manufactured goods. "Labor," in this economic sense, was both a type of activity and the people who undertook it. Here, too, connotations of earlier usages lived on. "Labor" remained something that was hard or even painful.

In late-nineteenth-century America, both terms acquired even newer meanings and connotations. "Capital" came increasingly to stand not merely for stock but for the owners of large enterprises, in particular corporations. "Labor" came to stand for associations of workers, for brotherhoods, and ultimately for unions. The struggle between "capital" and "labor" was therefore one between wealthy heads of industry and the variously organized men and women employed to do hard and dirty work.

In a whole string of controversies, capital and labor understood in these ways seemed to be viciously at each other's throats. In 1877, railroad strikes spread across Pennsylvania and Ohio and reached all the way to Chicago and St. Louis. Workers vented their anger by burning rail yards and derailing trains, and the owners organized special militia that opened fire on the strikers, their family members, and local supporters. In 1886, a strike against the McCormick Harvester Company in Chicago led to protests, rallies, and a fateful bombing in Haymarket Square. In 1892, the Carnegie Steel Company closed its massive plant in Homestead when a union of iron- and steelworkers refused to accept pay cuts and went on strike. Fierce fighting followed between the workers and Pinkerton forces hired by the company. In all of these controversies and others capital was likely to perceive the struggle as one between inventive and imaginative visionaries on the one hand and often unreliable workers on the other. Organized labor, meanwhile, might cast the struggle as one between greedy capitalist bosses and honest, hard-working citizens.

When push came truly to shove, law enforcement, the courts, the legislatures, and law itself had to intervene. Americans had long turned to law to understand and defuse social conflict, and in that sense law's assignment was not new. However, the assignment was now a more difficult one because of accelerating industrial development, the perception of polarization between "capital" and "labor," and the increasing friction between the two. Could law be a neutral director and adjudicator? Could the nation rely on a rule of law in an industrializing epoch that pitted capital and labor against each other?

This book will explore these questions with reference to the battle between capital and labor that dramatically capped the fractious industrializing era, the Pullman strike and boycott of 1894–95. The strike and boycott were more extended and convulsive than any others. Lines seemed fundamentally to be drawn, and worried Americans spoke of insurrection and rebellion. President Grover Cleveland ordered federal troops into the fray. Federal trial courts in many parts of the country considered both civil actions and criminal prosecutions involving the strikers, and the most important civil action from Chicago resulted in a celebrated and controversial appeal to the United States Supreme Court. The Pullman strike and boycott and the resulting trials and appeals are our best window on law's interaction with capital and labor in industrializing America. More generally, this story offers insights about the rule of law and about law itself.

———

I greatly appreciate the assistance of my wife, Elise Papke, on this book. Director of the Program in Public Health at Indiana University, she has frequently found time in her own busy schedule to read drafts and critique arguments. Our dialogue has greatly improved the book and, indeed, improves all of my work.

At Indiana University–Purdue University in Indianapolis, where I hold a joint appointment in the Schools of Law and Liberal Arts, many colleagues have expressed enthusiasm for my work. I received a summer research grant from the School of Law to work on the book and had superb support from School of Law librarians, especially Beverly Bryant, who pursued more books through interlibrary loan than she would like to remember. My assistant Vicky Grigsby provided invaluable help in word processing and in solving computer problems.

My research trips to Chicago in conjunction with the book most frequently led to the National Archives–Great Lakes Division, where the court records for the Pullman case are stored, and to the Harold Washington Library Center, home of excellent newspaper microfilm and local history collections. Archivists and librarians at both facilities were extraordinarily supportive of my work.

It has also been a delight to work with editors and staff at the University Press of Kansas. In particular, Michael Briggs encouraged me to pursue this study and provided advice in the shaping and completion of the manuscript. Two external readers of my initial manuscript offered valuable suggestions about ways to expand and improve the book.

The book is dedicated to my son, John Raymond Papke. He came into my home and became a wonderful part of my family during the two years in which I worked on the book. Elise, Tulita, Virginia, Nora, and I love him dearly.

CHAPTER I

Pullman, Debs, and Chicago in the 1890s

Chicago has been a symbol almost as long as it has been a place. Incorporated as a town in 1833 with a population of 350, the city experienced truly extraordinary growth during the nineteenth century. By 1870, it sprawled over 35 square miles and was home to three hundred thousand. Impressed by the city on the southwestern shore of Lake Michigan, Chicagoans and others saw Chicago as the symbol of the booming West and then the Midwest; as the emblem of American grit and growth; as the truest embodiment of the nation as a whole. The symbolic Chicago was the special place for the "American Dream" to come true.

During the 1870s still another notion joined the cavalcade of Chicago's symbolic identities: The city was now a phoenix as well. Chicago's Great Fire of 1871 killed almost three hundred people, destroyed eighteen thousand buildings, and left ninety thousand homeless, but in a way that never ceased to delight Chicagoans, the city then rolled up its sleeves and put itself back together again. In the next twenty years its corporate limits expanded to 185 square miles. Its population grew to five hundred thousand by 1880 and over a million by 1890. Like the mythological bird that rose from the ashes, Chicago soared. It passed Brooklyn and Philadelphia to the rank of second largest city in the land, after New York City.

Perhaps Chicago's location near systems of lake and river transport and its proximity to great stores of timber, iron, and coal made its dramatic growth and equally dramatic rebuilding inevitable, but the rebuilt Chicago was more complex than the earlier one. In the twenty years following the Great Fire, the city discarded even the suggestion of its recent small-town past. The *Chicago Tribune* noted in 1873 that one was lucky to recognize half the people at church or the theater, and "as to knowing one's neighbors, that has become a lost art." According to Bessie Louise Pierce, author of a multivolume history of Chicago, "Wealth became the main criterion of social standing." The gap between those so well off and gauche as to patronize a Palmer House barber shop with a floor of silver dollars and those struggling to survive in the dilapidated wooden shanty towns on the fringe of the city grew immense.

Chicago during the last quarter of the nineteenth century maintained its importance as a center for shipping and receiving and as a processor of agricultural goods, but the new Chicago also industrialized. Not only grain elevators but also smokestacks sprouted on its skyline. What's more, industrialization made Chicago a part of an interconnected modern economy. Local boosterism notwithstanding, Chicago became fully enmeshed in a national industrial system, one troubling to many social critics and one endlessly plagued by disputes between capital and labor.

The most extended and convulsive turmoil spawned by growth and industrialization in Chicago in the 1890s was the Pullman strike and boycott of 1894. The strike and boycott pitted prototypical representatives of "capital" and "labor": George M. Pullman, the chief stockholder and executive officer of a corporation manufacturing railroad cars, and Eugene V. Debs, a former railroad worker and president of the nation's largest railroad workers' union. The two are not the sole agents of the Pullman case. Their stories are just two among thousands in late-nineteenth-century Chicago. But by contemplating the careers and beliefs of Pullman and Debs, we can begin to appreciate the conflicting attitudes and interests that collided in Chicago and the nation in 1894. We can bring to life the notions of "capital" and "labor" that seemed to define the controversy and, in many ways, the entire industrializing era.

———

George Pullman came to Chicago from upstate New York, where his father had been a farmer, carpenter and—most notably—owner of a small business that physically relocated residential and business structures. As the years went by, Pullman's father increasingly concentrated his efforts on the building-moving business, and the business grew because of governmental decisions to widen the Erie Canal that stretched across upstate New York. Pullman's father even patented a machine for moving buildings on wheels, and the machine was no empty patent but rather functional and successful.

George Pullman himself was born on March 3, 1831. His parents' third child and third son, he finished only the fourth grade. Young George nevertheless became the apple of his father's eye, especially because George had a knack for business. He worked for three years in an uncle's general store and then settled into the role of the building-moving business's "trouble man." He contemplated what would not move. He recalculated lifts and angles. He crawled on the ground and muddied his clothes but then delighted in cleaning up, pomading his hair, and trooping about in a longtailed coat and dress hat.

Perhaps predictably, Pullman emerged among his siblings as the most likely heir to his father's predominant position. And indeed, when his father died in 1853, Pullman took control of the family business and almost immediately secured a lucrative contract with the State of New York to move twenty buildings, mostly warehouses, back from the Erie Canal right-of-way in Albion. Subsequent contracts followed, but, aware that not the Erie Canal but the related building-moving business would dry up, Pullman began investigating opportunities in other parts of the country.

In 1859 Pullman met with local officials and business proprietors in Chicago. The city was launching an effort to raise portions of the business district, which was built on swampy lands along Lake Michigan, to pave streets, and to install a sewage system. Pullman won the important contract to raise the five-story brick Matteson House, one of Chicago's most prominent hotels. Five foot seven, 160 pounds, and full of confidence, the twenty-eight-year-old Pullman was sure he could do the job. He moved to Chicago to lift the city and himself to new heights.

Using eight hundred coordinated screw jacks, Pullman efficiently raised the Matteson in only ten days. This success led to contracts to raise other downtown buildings and, on two separate occasions in 1860, even whole city blocks. Pullman himself was less and less likely to engage in physical work as the months went by. Grave bordering on severe, he was prone as a young man and throughout his life to blistering displays of temper. At least he reveled in his self-assigned role: standing in the street with a shrill whistle and tooting it each time the laborers were to turn the jacks under a building.

As was the case earlier along the banks of the Erie Canal, Pullman realized that his prospering business would not last forever. Chicago, he appreciated, would in fact rise from the swamp. Hence, Pullman investigated and launched a whole range of other ventures, including but not limited to small mines, sawmills, and freighting and haying operations in Colorado and elsewhere. The new venture that most captured his fancy and would come to dominate his later years was the manufacture and leasing of railroad cars.

Pullman's era was one of tremendous railroad expansion. Having started modestly in 1830 when Peter Cooper's locomotive *Tom Thumb* traveled thirteen miles on Baltimore and Ohio Railroad track, the American railroad system developed rapidly in the settled parts of the country. By 1850 the nation had nine thousand miles of track, and by 1860 the number had risen to thirty-one thousand. Substantial government land subsidies helped fuel the growth. Railroad owners replaced wooden tracks with iron rails and struggled to standardize track widths within their own lines and also with potential connecting lines. The standardization of track widths was one step on the way to merger and consolidation. In 1853 seven lines combined to become the New York Central, and in the same year the Pennsylvania Railroad began running directly from Philadelphia to Pittsburgh. By 1860 railroad lines had reached St. Joseph, Missouri, then the edge of the frontier. In a later era of interstate highways and travel by jet airplanes, it is easy to underestimate the great excitement the sight of a roaring, steaming train created for Americans of the 1850s. More fundamentally, railroads established themselves in the 1850s as models of modern organization and enterprise.

The most important changes wrought by the railroads of that decade may have involved the cost, speed, and range of raw material transport. However, Pullman was less interested in freight transport than in passenger travel. He used the railroads of the East and Midwest in his eager, ambitious pursuit of one business opportunity or another, but he did not enjoy rail travel. He knew special sleeping cars were beginning to appear, and on one occasion he booked a trip across New York simply to see how these cars measured up. He later reported how unsatisfactory they were. A man could bang his head on the car's low ceilings, Pullman said. To make matters worse, the cars had heat stoves that, given the lack of ventilation, resulted in an atmosphere that was "something dreadful." In his investigatory trip, Pullman purchased the top one of three bunks and climbed in fully clothed, as was expected. He could not sleep because he was uncomfortable, but staring at the car's ceiling not far from his face, he contemplated a better way to do things.

Pullman's first efforts to produce something better involved the Chicago, Alton and St. Louis Railroad, a smaller regional line. He persuaded the railroad company to give his ideas a try, and Pullman and the railroad company hired Leonard Seibert, a railroad mechanic, to reconstruct two conventional coaches as sleepers. Seibert gutted the coaches and refitted

4

them with cherry-wood interiors, closets, small box heaters, and oil lamps. Lower sleeping platforms could be fashioned from two seats, and upper berths were mounted close to the ceiling but then lowered at bedtime. The first use of the new cars took place on August 15, 1859, and they met with rave reviews. Some said the sleepers were comparable to cabins in a steamboat, in the 1850s the most luxurious way to travel.

Bolstered by early successes, Pullman manufactured more sleepers, developed dining and drawing room cars as well, and both sold and leased them all to a growing number of Midwestern railroad lines. Pullman's greatest strength was not managing his various small production plants, work he often left to his brother Albert and others. Instead, he continued to travel extensively to meet with railroad owners and to negotiate new contracts.

The Civil War itself seemed not to faze Pullman, and like other Northerners with money, he hired a substitute to take his place in the Union Army. However, at the end of the war Pullman did scramble to have his special cars included in the funeral train that carried Abraham Lincoln back to Illinois. A sales pitch was later crafted that asserted that the *Pioneer,* Pullman's fanciest car, was part of the train. Did Lincoln really have his penultimate rest in a Pullman berth? Historians have questioned whether the especially wide *Pioneer* could have squeezed past platforms and under bridges on the Springfield line.

Pullman's business activities of course had legal aspects, and the one that makes him especially representative of business in his era was the corporate charter he obtained from the Illinois legislature in 1867. Incorporation dated back to the beginning of the Republic, and as early as 1800 state governments had chartered roughly three hundred corporations. The numbers surged in subsequent decades, with the New England states proffering nineteen hundred corporate charters by 1830. As corporations increased in number, their identity and purpose also changed. The earliest corporations had a substantial degree of public purpose; some even perceived them as virtual agencies of the state governments. In the decades immediately before the Civil War, meanwhile, incorporation came to be purely a profit-seeking strategy. Would-be incorporators saw corporate charters as more of a right than a privilege with public responsibilities. Incorporation was available to anyone, and in some states the incorporation process was moved from the legislatures to early state licensing agencies.

Prior to the incorporation of his railroad car business, Pullman had run his various New York, Illinois, and Colorado businesses as either solely owned proprietorships or partnerships. With incorporation in 1867, the Pullman Palace Car Company came to have one thousand shares of stock, each of which originally sold for one hundred dollars. Pullman held five hundred of the shares, and at their first meeting the stockholders not surprisingly chose Pullman to be president and general manager. Surely the selections had been orchestrated in advance.

Later years would see the issuing of additional capital stock and various corporate restructurings of the Pullman Palace Car Company, and for both Pullman and American industry in general incorporation provided a great boon. In the traditional partnership, the partners formally agreed to work with one another for a set period of time, with each partner's personal assets vulnerable to claims against the partnership. A corporation, by contrast, afforded more permanence to the enterprise and also shielded founders and major stockholders from any personal liability for the corporation's debts and losses. The corporation thereby proved an extremely effective way to attract investors and, in the process, aggregate financing for large-scale ventures. More stable and more substantial than earlier partnerships, the corporation came quickly to be national as opposed to local or regional and to dominate, especially in the manufacturing sector. By 1900, corporations produced fully two-thirds of all United States manufactured goods.

In the early 1870s Pullman anguished as the Great Fire of 1871 completely destroyed the company offices in the downtown Armour Building and as the Panic of 1873 sank a bank in which he had heavily invested. But despite these setbacks, both Pullman and his corporation prospered. He temporarily consolidated his manufacturing operations at a larger plant in Detroit, negotiated new contracts with the Pennsylvania Railroad Company and various western lines, struck contracts in Mexico and Canada, and even launched less successful ventures in Europe. By 1879, the Pullman Palace Car Company boasted 464 cars, gross annual earnings of $2.2 million, and net annual earnings of almost $1 million.

During the 1880s, the company continued to grow. It leased specialty cars to many railroads, customarily agreeing to staff and repair the cars in return for fares and a two-cents-per-mile charge. The company also manufactured and sold freight, passenger, refrigerator, street, and elevated cars. By the early 1890s the company had a capitalization of over $36 million, and despite the ups and downs of the American economy, it had managed to pay robust quarterly dividends for over twenty years.

No puritanical workaholic, Pullman treated himself to the luxuries his wealth made possible. Still a clotheshorse, he ostentatiously courted the popular Hattie Sanger, the daughter of a construction company owner, and then dramatically married her alongside her father's deathbed. In 1876 the Pullmans moved into a newly constructed mansion on Chicago's fashionable Prairie Avenue. They raised four children and, despite Hattie's hypochondria, toured Europe and built summer homes on the St. Lawrence and in New Jersey. Traveling to the latter, one newspaper chided, required "a good many" Pullman cars to carry the family, twelve servants, five horses, three carriages, and a small mountain of bags, trunks, and furniture. President and Mrs. Grant called on the Pullmans in both Chicago and New Jersey, and the Pullmans spent a whole week as guests in the White House, where Mrs. Pullman joined Mrs. Grant as cohostess for two large receptions.

Pullman was a staunch Republican and contributed generously to the Republican Party, but he never sought elected office or a government position. Pullman's metier was business, and he ranked as one of the most prominent corporate leaders in not only Chicago but also the nation as a whole. The dominant ideology of the era credited the heads of corporations with great individual achievement, and many of these men, Pullman included, welcomed and promoted their own lionization. With chest puffed for all the world to see, Pullman developed a new corporate headquarters for the company in downtown Chicago. Located on the southwest corner of Michigan Avenue and Adams Street, the Pullman Building rose ten stories, featured a Gothic facade, and had all the most modern amenities, including, with a nod to the Great Fire of 1871, full fireproofing. Company offices occupied the first three floors of the building, and the dapper George Pullman could pop out the front door and enjoy lunch just across the street at the exclusive "millionaires' table" in the Chicago Club.

Eugene Debs was a generation younger than George Pullman, but the two men had roughly the same socioeconomic background. Debs's parents were Jean Daniel and Marguerite Marie Bettrich Debs, immigrants from Alsace. Marguerite Marie, or "Daisy" as she was known, had worked in a factory owned by Jean Daniel's father in Europe. They married across class lines and despite the objections of family members. After settling in Terre Haute, Indiana, the couple found some modest degree of success running a grocery store. They remained romantics, however, and readings of French novelists Eugene Sue and Victor Hugo were part of family life.

Their son Eugene Victor Debs was born on November 5, 1855, and his name reflected his parents' reading preferences. Three daughters, only two of whom survived, had preceded him. Other children followed. Daisy and Jean Daniel may have hoped Eugene would eventually take the reins of the family business or perhaps even move up the business ladder in their bustling town. But young Eugene lacked the calculating insights for business. Whenever he worked in the store, he rounded weights off in favor of customers and too liberally extended credit. In addition, Eugene did not take to school, finding the memorization and recitation of the era boring. To his petite-bourgeois parents' dismay, he quit school at fourteen and, like many young men of his era, went to work for the railroad. Handsome, gregarious, and industrious, he rode the rails to Chicago, to Evansville, and to St. Louis, moving up the ranks from laborer to painter to fireman.

After four years of adventure, Debs returned to Terre Haute. He supported himself working first as a billing clerk, but he remained active in railroad circles and especially in railroad brotherhoods. At first he was recording secretary of the local Brotherhood of Locomotive Firemen, and then he became editor of the national *Locomotive Firemen Magazine* and secretary-treasurer of the national organization. Debs championed the Protestant work ethic and civic responsibility, and the community of Terre Haute took him to be a respectable young man on the way up. He founded and led the local debating and lecture society; and in 1885 he married Kate Metzel, a local woman from a family much above his own in station. The marriage was childless and unhappy, but Debs continued to thrive in the public sphere. He was twice elected as a Democrat to the position of city clerk and also served a term in the Indiana legislature.

Of special interest are Debs's evolving views on organized labor. Labor organization during the 1880s and 1890s was diverse and fluid, and labor seemed to be searching for an institutional form that would effectively serve its interests in an industrial context. Craft unions, composed of skilled workers in a given trade, traced their lineage to the beginning of the nineteenth century. But no craft union ever enrolled as much as one-third of its trade, and craft union membership in the industrial sector as a whole never topped 10 percent of the workforce. The American Federation of

Labor (AFL), a national alliance of craft unions led by Samuel Gompers of the cigar makers, began its most dramatic growth in the late 1880s. The Knights of Labor, another prominent labor organization, began to decline about the time the AFL began to grow. Begun by garment cutters, the Knights of Labor under the leadership of machinist Terence Powderly recruited most types of workers, promoted producer cooperatives, and saw its membership peak at approximately 730,000 in 1886. Several abortive labor parties also attempted in the period to catch labor's eye, and some sections of the International Workingmen's Association, for which Karl Marx was a spokesman, were at least rambunctious, albeit nationally unsuccessful.

On this shifting spectrum of labor organizations, Debs originally came to rest on the right. His beloved railroad brotherhoods were relatively elite and exclusive workers' fraternities organized by craft. The Brotherhood of Locomotive Firemen was one of the most prestigious and successful, staking its claims to fame less on militant labor activity than on cheap insurance policies for members. Debs originally urged cooperation and conciliation with railroad capitalists, whom he early in his career called "architects of progress." Writing in an 1883 issue of *Locomotive Firemen's Magazine,* he said, "We do not believe in violence and strikes as means by which wages are to be regulated, but that all differences must be settled by mutual understanding arrived at by calm reasoning." In a burst of youthful vanity that had the potential to replay painfully in his mind in later years, Debs also boasted to brotherhood conventioneers that he had arranged "elegant sleeping cars" from none other than the Pullman Company.

Debs moved to the left—toward more inclusive union membership and more pronounced labor activism—in the late 1880s. The sobering defeat of Chicago's packinghouse workers in an 1885 labor dispute and subsequent defeats of striking railroad brotherhoods seem to have prompted changes in his thinking. In particular, the disastrous strike of 1888 against the Chicago, Burlington and Quincy Railroad, in which the firemen participated, led Debs to endorse a different variety of labor politics. On February 27, 1888, the engineers and the firemen with whom they closely worked struck the railroad. Management scurried to replace the striking workers with new men; realizing that the railroad might as a result be run without them, the engineers and firemen tried to bottle up the system with a boycott of all Burlington trains. The railroad filed suit to enjoin this strategy, and the courts agreed. Debs then watched in frustration as the injunction took its toll. Unemployed men eagerly took the jobs of the strikers. Members of other railroad brotherhoods walked through the engineers' and firemen's picket lines. The strike was broken, and railroad management crowed about putting the engineers and Debs's firemen in their place.

As a result of the totally unsuccessful strike, Debs came to believe and to argue that various types of railroad workers must work together against the railroads. He began to support the idea of "fraternal unity" and federation among the brotherhoods. "If corporations and the press confederate to overwhelm workingmen when they demand redress for grievances," he said, "they [the brotherhoods] too must federate to enforce their rights which corporations deny them when demands are made in a becoming manner." Federation, Debs seems to have thought, would actually end or prevent strikes because railroad owners and workers would see the need for arbitration.

Debs's belief in federation was not shared by all the brotherhoods, which had a hierarchy of their own and also tended to look down upon unskilled laborers. Hence, an irritated Debs left the brotherhoods to become president of the American Railway Union, a new labor organization that was founded in Chicago on June 20, 1893. Membership in the union was open to any Caucasians who worked for a railroad, regardless of their specific jobs. The union included locals as well as a national office. Ten individuals or more employed in railroad service could form a local and automatically affiliate with the national union. The latter, meanwhile, had departments of literature and education, legislation, cooperation, mediation, and insurance.

While the earlier brotherhoods emphasized cooperation, the American Railway Union was more confrontational. Large numbers of railroad workers joined in late 1893 and early 1894, and in the spring of 1894 the union effectively struck the Great Northern Railroad, which had ordered three pay reductions in the span of only eight months. James J. Hill, the owner of the Great Northern, agreed to arbitration, and this victory brought even more members into Debs's union.

Debs had reason to feel vindicated. Brotherhood leaders had ridiculed him when he turned to the American Railway Union. Now, less than a year after its founding, the union had established 465 locals and signed up 150,000 workers—figures that dwarfed those of any single brotherhood. Debs had become one of the nation's most prominent labor leaders, and many thought industrial unionism of the sort he represented would bring workers the pay and respect they deserved. Journeying to his beloved Terre Haute for a rest, Debs savored the scene when he left St. Paul after the victory over the Great Northern. Railroad workers stood on both sides of the tracks, some crying and some pumping their shovels in the air. "That tribute was more precious to me," Debs said later, "than all of the banquets in the world."

———

George Pullman and Eugene Debs, the actual and connotative representatives of capital and labor, clashed in Pullman, Illinois—the company town on the southern outskirts of Chicago that Pullman developed for his workers. Pullman began planning the town in 1879, and his plans became a reality when the town opened on January 1, 1881. Located on a previously unincorporated tract near Lake Calumet, the town was not a municipality in the normal sense but just a two-square-mile tract of private property, maintained and rented out by the company.

Countless hours went into the design of Pullman. Perhaps most strikingly, the housing reflected workplace hierarchy. Freestanding homes were for executives, row houses for skilled or at least senior workers, tenements for unskilled workers, and a cluster of rooming houses for common laborers. Workers did not have to live in town, and with rents averaging fourteen dollars per month, well above the working-class norm, a good number chose to rent in nearby towns. Pullman, meanwhile, was sure his brick structures with cellars, gas and water, and brightly painted interiors were well worth the price. He also helped ensure the rents were paid by issuing each tenant two checks—one for the amount of rent and the other for remaining wages. A paymaster delivered the checks with a rent collector in tow, and workers were encouraged to immediately endorse and hand back the rent check.

In addition to homes, the town included an arcade for merchants, an approved church, and a hotel named after Pullman's favorite child, his daughter Florence. Like Pullman's housing, space in the arcade and even in the church was rented. The library in the former, full of books carefully selected by the company, was a bit of a bust. In a workforce of, at one point, over 4000, only 250 paid the three-dollar annual fee for privileges. The church and its parsonages were also underutilized, and sometimes vacant, because the rent was higher than most churches could pay. The Hotel Florence included a special suite for Pullman's use, but on most nights he chose to return to his mansion on Prairie Avenue.

On the northern edge of town was the community's true heart, the company's new production plant. Always resourceful, Pullman used shavings from the plant's carpentry shops to fuel the boilers and exhaust water from the boilers to fill the artificial Lake Vista. Pumps even sent sewage from the plant and homes to a farm three miles away, where it became fertilizer on a Pullman farm that grew vegetables, which were in turn sold to Pullman workers. The scheme, Pullman told a reporter, was "simplicity itself—we are landlord and employers. That is all there is of it."

In reality, there was more. Pullman wanted through his town to convey and promote a vision of how the industrial workplace and society as a whole should function. Although he fell back on simpler characterizations of the town of Pullman when these characterizations served his interests, the successful industrialist had a decided sense of how things should be done. The "Pullman way" was a social vision in which he was personally and financially invested.

Pullman incessantly promoted his model town and the vision it embodied through both the written text and photography. In the late nineteenth century the latter was still used primarily for portraiture and only rarely for advertising, but the Pullman Company employed a full-time photographer and in 1888 set up a photography department that kept abreast of the most recent photographic technology. Between 1883 and 1893, the company published four small but still spectacular books on the car works and the town, all suggesting that developments in both were pathbreaking. Newspapers and magazines drew from the Pullman publications and photographs, and the company itself distributed thousands of the publications and photographs during the 1893 World's Fair in Chicago.

The town of Pullman, the company and its founder George Pullman suggested, would have an "ennobling and refining" effect, and the town would attract a superior type of workman, disinclined to sloppy work, shirking on the job, and absenteeism. Pullman wanted his workers to manifest "habits of respectability," that is, good manners, neatness, cleanliness, and sobriety. There were no brothels or saloons in town, and Pullman officials reminded tenants if their conduct or homes were out of line. Even the plays performed at the town theater were selected with an eye to inculcating proper conduct and values. To help shore up the enterprise, Pullman preferred as workers fair-haired Northern Europeans and so-called "buckwheats" from rural America, while the Irish were disfavored. Leases allowed Pullman to bump out with only ten days notice those who did not measure up. Thankful, deferential, well-policed workers, Pullman assumed, would serve as models for the American labor force in general.

In retrospect, the whole project was an immense exercise in hubris, and the Pullman workers, not surprisingly, did not always understand things in the way Pullman wanted. Thirsty workers may not have been able to buy a drink in town, for example, but they beat hasty paths to the saloons in nearby towns. The population, which reached eighty-six hundred by 1885, was more ambitious and younger than the average workforce, and many residents wanted to "move up" by purchasing homes—something that was impossible in Pullman itself. Most generally, many of the workers grumbled and complained behind closed doors.

Perhaps the best and most extensive treatment of Pullman in the era came from Richard Ely, a professor of economics from Johns Hopkins University, who published an article about Pullman in the February 1885 issue of *Harper's Monthly*. Ely realized that the town was not simply a company town designed to concentrate and efficiently utilize labor. He appreciated that a social vision was being developed and promoted as well, and he was prepared to scrutinize it. In order to do so, Ely had to engage in something comparable to later-day investigative journalism. He had at his disposal Pullman's public relations materials and even used some of the company's photographs in *Harper's*, but he wanted more than what the company provided. Since all the Pullman enterprises "are conducted with what seems to the writer a needless air of secrecy," Ely complained, "reliable statistics are obtained with difficulty."

Setting up what would ultimately be his negative conclusions, Ely began his article by acknowledging the surface wonders of the town of Pullman. "Very gratifying is the impression of the visitor who passes hurriedly through Pullman and observes only the splendid provision for the present material comforts of the residents," Ely said. "What is seen in a walk or drive through the streets is so pleasing to the eye that a woman's first exclamation is certain to be, 'Perfectly lovely!'" Ely went on to comment on the cheerful surroundings and tidy homes, none with old clothes stuffed into broken windows as was common in dirty American industrial cities. He observed with favor the absence of barns and praised the modern sewage system and bustling shopping arcade. He acknowledged the relatively high wages. But really, he wondered, did this town live up to its goal of being a "forerunner of better things for the laboring classes"?

The answer, Ely said, was no. The most serious problem was that the Pullman Company owned and ran everything. "With the exception of the management of the public school, every municipal act is here the act of a private corporation." As a result, nobody regarded Pullman as a real home; residing there was "like living in a great hotel." "It is indeed a sad spectacle," Ely said.

> Here is a population of eight thousand souls where not one single resident dare speak out openly his opinion about the town which he lives in. One feels that one is mingling with a dependent, servile people. There is an abundance of grievances, but if there lives in Pullman one man who would give expression to them in print over his own name, diligent inquiry continued for ten days was not sufficient to find him.

"In looking over all the facts of the case," Ely said in conclusion, "the idea of Pullman is un-American." Ely likened George Pullman to the German kaiser or Russian czar. The town was "benevolent, well-wishing feudalism, which desires the happiness of people, but in such a way as shall please the authorities." We might hope that Pullman had inaugurated a "new era in the history of labor," but if this new era was to "immesh our laborers in a net-work of communities owned and managed by industrial superiors, then let every patriotic American cry, 'God forbid!'" What Pullman truly represented, Ely growled, was the "establishment of the most absolute power of capital, and the repression of all freedom."

George Pullman's worst fear might have been that the self-protective servility of his workers would give way to labor organization and activism. Labor unions and labor unrest would expose his vision even more than did Richard Ely's article. And indeed, in hopes of maintaining peace on capital's terms, Pullman had never recognized that labor unions could have a place in his company or town. In the early years of the town, workers told a commission appointed by President Grover Cleveland to look into the strike, the company discharged anyone who joined a union.

Pullman subscribed to a late-nineteenth-century variety of "free labor" ideology. This ideology, which had taken hold in the North in the decades immediately preceding the Civil War, stressed the way honest, diligent, sober labor could and did lead to economic independence. Free labor produced a republic of independent farm owners and business proprietors, and, ideologically speaking, northern society as a result was superior to the slave society of the South. The victory of the North in the Civil War further established the dominance of free labor ideology, but its central thrust changed somewhat in the context of accelerating industrialization. Wage labor for many had obviously ceased to be a temporary condition on the way to becoming an independent merchant or farmer. But the laborer was still "free" in that he could theoretically choose his employer and contract for wages and working conditions as he saw fit. With corporate control of the industrial sector growing dramatically, the laborer did not really have economic autonomy, but his choice of employer and labor contract remained noncoerced.

Surveying his company and town, Pullman honestly believed his workers could accept or reject work as they saw fit. His relationship with each worker was voluntary and contractual. Pullman wanted to buy labor on certain terms, and some workers were willing to sell it on those same terms. Each party was a free-willed citizen and exercised freedom of choice in agreeing to the contract they struck. However, that was as far as things went. The labor contract had no guaranteed duration. If Pullman did not approve of a worker's efforts or if economic conditions dictated a reduction in the workforce, Pullman could renegotiate the terms of employment or even release the worker. The workers, Pullman thought, also had their options. If they tired of their employment or perceived better opportunities, they could terminate their contract. They could freely move on to another position.

Nothing suggests that Pullman was disingenuous in his conceptualization of the labor contract, but even in his own times his thinking was somewhat fusty. Some other employers emphasized not the agreement between employer and worker but rather market standards. The price of labor, they thought, would be determined by what the market would bear. Supply and demand ruled. Then, too, labor itself was beginning to articulate critiques of the Pullmanesque variety of free labor ideology and the market standard. In an age of accelerating industrialization and corporate control, workers had an unequal and extremely vulnerable position. Employers set the terms of employment, and workers also had no power and choice in the wildly fluctuating economy.

Unfortunately for Pullman, he was unable to insulate his company and town from visions other than his own. The nation as a whole and adjacent Chicago in particular were convulsed with labor controversy. The local

Knights of Labor had conducted a vigorous campaign for an eight-hour working day, which culminated in a one-day strike of sixty thousand Chicago workers. In addition, a bitter strike raged in 1886 at the huge McCormick reaper factory. After police charged a line of union members trying to prevent "scabs" from taking their jobs, killing two and wounding others in the process, labor groups organized a rally at Haymarket Square not far from downtown Chicago. At the rally a bomb exploded, killing seven and injuring sixty-seven. Police arrested union leaders and especially anarchists, and eventually courts steeped in fear and political paranoia convicted eight anarchists of the bombing.

Against this backdrop, it would have been amazing if the Pullman workers had not become agitated. They engaged in several small walkouts in specific departments in the early 1880s, and then in 1886 a full-scale strike occurred. The workers' demands included the eight-hour day but stressed even more the terms and conditions of their specific work environment. The workers were angered that Pullman had taken many of the men off wages and placed them instead on piecework. For Pullman, this was a way to increase production and an "educational tool in that it offered incentive to the worker to improve his skill." For the workers, it seemed just a way to squeeze more effort out of them. In addition, they pointed to inequities among the rates for different shops and trades, a complaint indicative of something less than full worker solidarity and reminiscent of the squabbling Debs had encountered in the brotherhoods. Pullman workers were also unhappy that the company had discontinued its practice of automatically paying workers for days lost due to injuries on the job.

Lurking in the 1886 strike was a view of labor-capital relations quite different from the one held by Pullman. Not all workers had this alternative view, and, as previously noted, in late-nineteenth-century America only a minority of workers belonged to unions. However, some workers had come to recognize the desirability and potential power of what has come to be called "collective bargaining." They thought workers should be consulted collectively as to wages, working conditions, and dismissals. The labor contract should not be determined by the imbalanced power differential of the worker-employer relationship or by capital's wishes for profit in the market context. Give workers the power to speak as a group to employment matters. If they could not speak, a strike was one way to express demands and preferences. Through a strike, workers could rattle the cage, and maybe employers would hear the rattling.

Pullman was saddened by the strike. He offered to open his books to a workers' committee to show that changes regarding piecework and workplace injuries were necessary. At the same time, Pullman refused to let the workers set policy in *his* company and *his* town. In the end, he reopened his plant with heavy police protection, and most of the workers grudgingly returned to their jobs.

Between 1887 and 1893 the town of Pullman's population grew to over twelve thousand, and although a deep sense of harmony did not reign, only a few short-lived labor disputes occurred in the town and its shops. Then, in the late summer of 1893, the national economic depression caught up with Pullman. The company had been spared for several months by the unusual demand for cars prompted by the Columbian Exposition, Chicago's World's Fair. Now, with the exposition ending, many of the shops stood idle, and Pullman approved firings, layoffs, and wage reductions.

Behind the scenes, Pullman also accepted contracts at a loss in hopes of preserving jobs. He also launched extensive servicing and repair operations as well as plant renovations in hopes of keeping the workers on the job, and he closed his smaller plant in Detroit in order to preserve work and resources for the company's town. But even these steps received a mixed reaction from the workers. According to the Reverend William H. Carwardine, a Methodist minister in Pullman and, most decidedly, not a company man, the workers "had never seen any evidences of paternal love on the part of Mr. Pullman in his previous dealings with them." They could not "disabuse their minds of the thought that perhaps he was keeping the shops open, and taking work at a loss in order to get his returns in rent."

In the spring of 1894, after the American Railway Union's victory over the Great Northern, some 35 percent of the Pullman workforce joined the union. The workers were eligible for membership because roughly twenty miles of track ran into or through the company's car works, and the union charter said anyone working in any capacity on railroad lines could join. Debs may not have anticipated that manufacturing rather than railroad workers would join the union, but he had promoted industrywide membership so that the railroads could not turn one group of workers against another.

With union membership inspiring more confidence and aggressiveness, the workers continued to complain about layoffs, wage reductions, and the company's refusal to lower rents and gas and water charges. The workers were also irritated that foremen and company officers still drew high salaries and that the company kept paying quarterly dividends to stockholders. If the company was in such dire straits, they wondered, why were the workers the only ones suffering?

At the beginning of May, the workers' grievance committee, headed by Thomas Heathcoate, presented its complaints to the company. A fifty-eight-year-old skilled inside finisher who had worked at Pullman for five years, Heathcoate was not an irascible firebrand, but the company did not respond well to him. In a meeting at the company's headquarters in downtown Chicago, Thomas H. Wickes, a Pullman vice president, asked for a written summary of the grievances. On May 9, at a second meeting, George Pullman himself appeared. He pointed out that he had tried to keep the shops open even at a loss, and as he had done in 1886, he offered to open his books. He wanted to demonstrate to Heathcoate and his committee the company's plight. However, Pullman insisted that he could not restore wages to higher levels, and he categorically refused to lower rents in the model town. Rents, he said, had nothing to do with wages. Unless one would argue that rents could also be fixed in the neighboring towns of Kensington and Roseland, he said, one should not argue that the Pullman Company should disregard the normal rules of supply and demand that govern rents and landlord-tenant relations in general.

The workers were unwilling to differentiate Pullman the employer from Pullman the landlord, and most thought Pullman's position on rents was at least in part disingenuous. Comparable housing was in fact cheaper in Kensington and Roseland, but workers felt some need to remain in Pullman to protect their jobs and move up the ladder. The company, it seems, had a policy of laying off last those workers who were Pullman tenants. Workers also told the United States Strike Commission that promotions were made contingent on moving into Pullman housing.

After the meetings with Wickes and Pullman, several members of the grievance committee were dismissed from their jobs. The company denied it was retaliating against them, but the workers were more than dubious. Representatives of the workers met into the wee hours of May 11 at Turner Hall in nearby Kensington. After heated arguments full of anxiety and frustration, the committee members voted 42–4 to strike.

On the morning of May 11 the workers reported to the shops, but when given the call by their leaders, the workers walked out. The strikers claimed that 4,300 workers were employed at the beginning of the strike and that only 300 were willing to keep working. The company countered with claims that only 2,850 were employed and 600 wanted to keep working. Whatever the case, the factory became ominously still, and company representatives hastily posted a notice on the gates that read: "The works are closed until further notice."

Pullman considered the strike an affront to his judgment, honesty, and right to employ labor on the terms he considered fair and appropriate. He also expressed surprise. "I believed the men were satisfied with the arrangements," he said, "and I was quite unprepared for the announcement that they had left work." Beginning a public relations battle that would rage alongside the strike itself, Pullman also asserted, "The condition of the men was better than that of any body of workingmen in this or any other country."

Technically speaking, the strike was not as yet a strike by the American Railway Union, but union officials had been in Pullman and in the meetings in Turner Hall in Kensington during the days immediately preceding the strike. Eugene Debs rushed to Pullman from union business outside of the state. Although he worried that the availability of unemployed workers would make the strike difficult to win, he had previously deplored the workers' subsistence living conditions and indebtedness to Pullman. Once on the scene, Debs bitterly vented his feelings in an address to the workers. Pullman, Debs thought, was a "a rich plunderer," and he called on workers "to strip the mask of hypocrisy from the pretended philanthropist and show him to the world as an oppressor of labor." "The paternalism of Pullman," Debs said, "is the same as the interest of a slave holder in his human chattels. You are striking to avert slavery and degradation."

One might have expected that the industrial epoch's titanic struggle between capital and labor would come about in other places and in other ways. To some extent, the affiliation of the Pullman workers with the American Railway Union was a fluke. But regardless of this, Chicago and the nation had before it a conflict of capital and labor that would take on massive proportions. Chicago, so proud of its symbolic significance, was now to add another notable event to its history. The Pullman strike and related legal cases would make Chicago the chief site of the most significant power struggle between capital and labor in industrial America.

CHAPTER 2

The Strike and Boycott

Historical events and developments are not inevitable, but something invisible seemed at times to be expanding the Pullman strike into an immense battle between capital and labor. The membership rules of the American Railway Union had opened the door for the Pullman workers, and a serendipitous union convention in Chicago subsequently allowed delegates to observe the Pullman situation firsthand. The delegates decided to boycott Pullman cars, and the boycott spread like wildfire across the nation. Railroads that leased or bought Pullman cars resisted the boycott, and the strike that led to a boycott became even larger as railroad workers retaliated against their employers.

Eventually, President Grover Cleveland called out federal troops to restore order and clear the way for railroad traffic, and federal courts in Chicago and elsewhere were asked to intervene. Subsequent chapters will explore in detail developments in the courtroom arena, but the strike and boycott themselves first deserve attention. They were front-page stories in the nation's newspapers for several months in the spring and summer of 1894, and they left the nation damaged, perplexed, and profoundly concerned about its future.

After the Pullman workers boisterously marched out of the shops and began their strike on May 11, almost no disorder or violence occurred in the town of Pullman itself. The *Daily Inter Ocean,* an excellent Chicago newspaper of the period, reported, "No one would have guessed a great strike was on from the appearance of the pretty streets in Pullman.... Women, children, and men passed up and down the avenues enjoying the sunshine." Many of the workers gathered at the baseball fields along Lake Calumet, and when "the striking laundry girls, 173 in number" showed up at the fields, they were greeted with special respect and enthusiasm.

Having already deemed the labor stoppage "the most remarkable strike in the history of the country," the *Daily Inter Ocean* was amazed by "the awesome stillness" that reigned all about the town. Pullman seemed "as quiet as a New England village, and there was nothing to indicate that the workers in the car shops were in the throes of a strike fever." Even a month into the strike, it seemed to the newspaper that "It is rather as though each day was a Sunday, all is so quiet and solemn and orderly."

The eerie calm and peacefulness were not flukes. Sensitive to public relations concerns, Thomas Heathcoate, members of the strike committee, and representatives of the American Railway Union urged the workers to conduct themselves like gentlemen and to abide by the law. American Railway Union vice president George W. Howard said in an address at Turner Hall in Kensington, "Now, men, you have work before you, and you must do it like American citizens. Use no threats, no intimidations, no force toward anyone who goes into the works." In particular, Howard added, "Let liquor of all kinds alone. If you drink at all, you are liable to lose your senses, and if you lose your senses, God knows what will happen."

Even the huge car works on the northern edge of town escaped damage. The Reverend Carwardine called attention to this and cast the workers' conduct as a "model strike." Throughout May and into June, he said, "not the slightest unusual infringement of law had taken place." Both sides took credit. The workers pointed to the ring of three hundred men it had stationed around the plant to prevent hoodlums and rowdies from damaging Pullman property. The Pullman Company said the workers' claim to be guarding the property was a mere pretense. Really, the workers were picketing and particularly determined to prevent anyone from going to work in the plant. If there was limited destruction and violence, George Pullman asked, should not "some credit be given to the administration of the Company, which prohibits drinking saloons, and provides various sources of elevation of character?"

Pullman hoped that the strike would collapse quickly like the one of 1886, but the workers received support that helped them hold out. The Secord-Hopkins trading company, which counted among its partners a former Pullman employee, contributed twenty-five thousand pounds of beef and an equal amount of flour. It also furnished a large room that could be used to care for the sick and injured. Physicians donated their services, and Chicago unions and organizations established a strike fund that at one point grew to fifteen thousand dollars. The biggest contributors were the painters, carpenters, and typographical workers, but the 34th Ward Republican Club, the United Turner Societies, the people of Hammond, Indiana, and the 14th Precinct police station also made substantial contributions. Individuals of modest means also dropped off provisions, including everything from a box of hats to a single caddy of chewing tobacco.

The true center of strike activity was the Turner Hall in nearby Kensington, where the strike committee held meetings open to the press and public. The strikers and their supporters, following a suggestion from Debs, wore small white ribbons, and they rallied almost nightly. Debs, Howard, and other officers from both the American Railway Union and other labor organizations addressed the rallies. In a talk on May 14 Debs promised the workers he was with them "heart and soul." "As a general thing," he said, "I am against a strike, but when the only alternative to a strike is the sacrifice of rights, then I prefer to strike. I am free to confess that I do not like the paternalism of Pullman. He is everlastingly saying, 'What can we do for our poor workingmen?'" This "interrogation," Debs thought, was an insult, and he won thunderous applause by announcing the real question was, "What can we do for ourselves?"

While the workers wore their white ribbons to rallies in Kensington, company officials and their supporters—admittedly a smaller group—wore miniature American flags and used the Hotel Florence as their gathering place. The flag symbol offended many of the workers. Some were Civil War veterans, and an even larger number were the proud children of veterans. As self-conscious patriots, they resented the symbolic implication that the other side was somehow more "American."

Company spokesmen were much less rhetorical than labor spokesmen, and much of the time the company tried to maintain a dignified silence, to in effect rise above the controversy. "This is not an issue that can be thrashed out in the papers," Pullman vice president Thomas Wickes said. The company continued to reject arbitration, even when asked to consider it by Chicago's mayor, the city's common council, the eminent citizens of the Civic Federation, and Mayor Pingree of Detroit. The latter was himself a major manufacturer and claimed to have telegrams from fifty other mayors urging arbitration.

"We just cannot afford in the present state of commercial depression to pay higher wages than we were paying," Wickes said. "We would prefer rather to close our works for six months than to run them, which we would have to do if we paid higher wages, at a loss." What's more, Wickes added in a somewhat more menacing tone, the company had always planned ahead and had "a large excess of rolling stock on hand." "The truth," Wickes thought, was that "the Pullman Company had in the past, when times were better, been paying the men such a high rate of wages that now that the conditions were altered, they could not accustom themselves to it."

———

As part of what seemed the inevitable expansion of the controversy, the American Railway Union's representatives gathered in Chicago for the union's first national convention about one month after the strike began. Roughly four hundred delegates met in Uhlich Hall, and with memories of the Great Northern victory still fresh, optimism reigned. Debs was clearly the union's leader, and not only the delegates but also members of the Chicago press wanted to meet with him. Always gregarious and also fond of alcohol, Debs obliged one and all.

Privately, meanwhile, Debs realized that the Pullman strike was a cloud on the union's horizon. Although genuinely sympathetic to the plight of the Pullman workers, he continued to worry that the nation's economic depression and abundance of unemployed workers could undermine strike efforts. He knew Pullman could find men willing to take the jobs of strikers. Debs warned the conventioneers to proceed cautiously with regard to the Pullman strike and in general.

Few listened. Given the fame of the model town and the notoriety of the strike, union conventioneers could not resist visiting Pullman. Once there, the conventioneers were moved by the plight of the striking workers and their families. The conventioneers constituted themselves a committee of the whole, and on June 15 they received a lengthy report by Pullman workers. The report alleged that wage reductions were 30 to 70 percent while corporate dividends remained at previous levels. The report also underscored the irksome fact that Pullman had refused to lower rents. Yes, the workers admitted, Pullman had evicted no one for failure to pay their rent or utility bills, but this, the workers thought, was just part of Pullman's effort to win public favor. "We struck at Pullman because we were without hope," the report said. "Twenty thousand souls, men, women, and little ones, have their eyes turned toward this convention today, straining eagerly through despondency for a glimmer of the heaven-sent message you alone can give us on this earth."

Among the most effective of the convention speakers was Pullman seamstress Jennie Curtis. She was the president of the "girls' union local" in Pullman, and along with the other women made carpets, drapes, linen, and seat coverings for the Pullman cars. Her father had worked for the Pullman company for thirteen years. When he died, Curtis angrily reported, the Company demanded she assume responsibility for the sixty dollars he owed in back rent. Deductions for the rent were taken from her biweekly paycheck. The check itself then totaled between nine dollars and ten dollars, and she paid seven dollars of that for room and board in Pullman. "We ask you," she said passionately to the convention, "to come along with us because we are not just fighting for ourselves, but for decent conditions for workers everywhere."

The idea of boycotting railroads using Pullman cars surfaced; indeed, from the very beginning of the strike individual American Railway Union locals in St. Paul and elsewhere had sporadically cut out Pullman cars. But union officers and convention delegates knew this was a drastic step. Sympathy existed in Chicago and the nation for the Pullman workers. They were common men and women outmuscled by a powerful employer and landlord. Yet a boycott affecting the railroads might be a different matter. While many could appreciate the validity of a labor union and the propriety of a strike, fewer considered boycotting appropriate. Unlike a direct strike, a boycott was an indirect weapon and would hurt other companies as well as shippers, passengers, and average citizens. Debs himself said he did "not really like the term 'boycott.' . . . There is a deep-seated hostility in the country to the term 'boycott.'"

Instead of boycotting, the convention delegates decided to approach George Pullman with still another request for arbitration. They selected a committee of twelve, including Jennie Curtis and five other delegates from Pullman, and the committee met with Thomas Wickes. The latter refused to negotiate in any way with the American Railway Union, saying the company was willing only to meet with its own workers as individuals. Six selected Pullman workers—ostensibly a group of individuals—then went back to Wickes for a second meeting, but he refused to discuss wages with them or even to consider the possibility of arbitration. Wickes, in fact, told the six that they should consider themselves not employees but rather former employees, who "stood in the same position as the man on the sidewalk."

Pullman did not participate in the meetings, but Wickes's rigid position on arbitration came from his boss. In a later statement for the *New York Tribune,* Pullman asked with the rigid logic so offensive to the workers how he, as the head of the Pullman Company, could allow a body of men not concerned with the interests of the company's shareholders to decree that the workmen should be employed at wages greater than their work could be sold for. "Who will deny that such a question is plainly not a subject of arbitration?" he said. The "real question," Pullman was sure, involved "the possibility of the creation and duration of a dictatorship, which could make all the industries of the United States and the daily comfort of the millions dependent upon them, hostages for the granting of any fantastic whim of such a dictator. Any submission by him would have been a long step in that direction, and in the interest of every law-abiding citizen of the United States was not to be considered for a moment."

Gathered for their daily meetings in Uhlich Hall on North Clark Street, the convention delegates were at a loss regarding what to do. They passed a resolution commending Chicago mayor John P. Hopkins for contributing $1500 to the strike fund. They decided to transfer $2000 from the union's general fund to the Pullman strike fund and to assess all union members ten cents per week to aid the Pullman cause. They self-righteously voted to give Jennie Curtis a gold watch. Through it all, they hoped somehow Pullman would give an inch.

Finally, on June 22, six weeks after the start of the strike, the convention took the step it had hesitated to take earlier. It passed a motion to refuse to handle Pullman cars or any trains with Pullman cars unless by June 26 the company responded to grievances. Once the motion passed, the convention voted again to make the decision unanimous. The delegates then jumped from their chairs and cheered lustily, one assumes in a combination of bravado and anxiety.

The hope, actually, was that this step would compel the railroads to boycott the Pullman Company, but from the start, the press and public did not take to heart this nuanced understanding. The *Daily Inter Ocean* declared, "The railroad strike now on is one of the most foolish and inequitous ever ordered in this country.... It is arbitrary, arrogant, and without a shadow of justification." Others agree that the union was in fact the boycotter. When three delegates once again trooped to Wickes's office to tell him of the decision, he informed them bluntly that the company would not listen to the grievances, enter into arbitration, or have any dealings with representatives of the union.

———

After the boycott had been authorized by the convention delegates, the American Railway Union polled its lodges to see if they would support the plan. Each and every one supported the boycott enthusiastically, a reaction that might seem surprising since few of the lodges had any extensive contact with the Pullman Company. Evident here and elsewhere was the more general anger of the railroad workers and their dissatisfaction with their wages, working conditions, company blacklists, and humiliating treatment. The boycott, it would become obvious, was fueled not merely by the conduct of the Pullman Company or by solidarity with the Pullman workers who had joined the American Railway Union. The boycott tapped the deep and pervasive alienation of labor in general. Workers were mad about their situation. They were angry about their limited opportunities and about what they took to be the mean and arbitrary treatment they received from the distant owners of the industries in which they worked.

Crucial to the effectiveness of the boycott would be the switchmen, and as fate would have it, switchmen had joined the union in especially large numbers. Debs predicted to the convention that, in keeping with the plan, loyal switchmen would refuse both to add Pullman cars to trains and to remove them. They would simply not handle them. The railroads would then dismiss the switchmen and try to replace them, which would lead fellow union members to walk out in solidarity with the switchmen. This would bring still more trains to a halt.

The boycott began slowly but then progressed almost exactly as Debs anticipated. By June 27, one day after the deadline for the Pullman Company had passed, five thousand men had left their jobs, and fifteen railroads were tied up. By the next day, forty thousand men had gone out, and rail traffic was affected on almost all rail lines west of Chicago. By the next day, almost one hundred thousand men were on strike, and at least twenty railroads were tied up or completely stopped. The union had few lodges in the East and Old South, but the boycott was remarkably effective everywhere else.

Although he had predicted what would happen, Debs seemed stunned by the anger the boycott had flushed out. He sent telegram after telegram to local lodges, urging them to avoid violence and to stop no trains. He reiterated that the union was merely refusing to handle Pullman cars and was not on strike against all railroads. And he declined an offer from the Knights of Labor to call a general strike in Chicago. The press had already dubbed events the "Debs Rebellion," and Debs realized how close things were to spinning out of control.

Pullman decided to deal with the deteriorating situation by, of all things, leaving Chicago. He moved his servants to places of safety, stored his best china in vaults in the Pullman Building, and placed an armed guard around his Prairie Avenue mansion. On June 28, he and his family set out for their mansion on the New Jersy shore, and from there he traveled to Castle Rest, his home on the St. Lawrence River at the Thousand Islands. He declared to the press that the whole matter was now out of his hands.

Despite Pullman's declarations, of course, his company and individual railroads attempted to counter the boycott. Even more important were the collective efforts of the railroads through the General Managers' Association. An organization of twenty-four railroads with terminals in Chicago, the General Managers' Association had since its formation in 1886 attempted to standardize local switching, loading, and weighing. The managers' group in 1892 had established a wage scale for Chicago switchmen, and they had also proposed elaborate wage schedules that the member railroads might use on their entire lines. The schedules were not mandatory, but they aided individual lines in negotiations with workers and even began to serve as a national wage scale of sorts for railroad workers. Perhaps most significantly for what lay ahead, the managers' association in 1893 had begun helping individual roads find replacement workers when the roads' own workers struck. With a combined capital stock of $818 million, 41,000 miles of track, and 221,000 employees, the railroads represented in the General Managers' Association were a formidable foe for Debs and the American Railway Union.

With Chicago's Rookery Hall as their base, the managers' group prepared to fight. They refused to communicate with Debs or the union, but through the press and other sources they of course knew just what was threatened. On June 26, the first day of the boycott, Everett St. John, the chairman of the managers' association, announced that the boycott would be resisted to the fullest. John M. Egan, the one-time general manager of the Chicago and Great Western Railroad, was designated as the coordinator of the antiboycott effort. Egan chaired daily closed meetings for the managers' group, and the latter took their first steps: They hired a passel of lawyers to look into the legal aspects of the controversy, and they allocated funds for an even larger number of detectives, who were to collect and report names of boycott-supporting employees.

Throughout the East—in Baltimore, Philadelphia, Pittsburgh, Buffalo, and New York—the managers' group began recruiting strikebreakers, and as Debs had feared all along, there was no shortage of unemployed men willing and available to work. Indeed, some of them apparently held grudges as a result of past labor controversies. Recruits in New York felt that many current railroad workers had grabbed their jobs during an earlier strike against the Gould lines. "We are going to settle an old account," one strikebreaker said. "The men who are striking now are the men who helped to fill our places then. Now we are going west to take their jobs." The managers' group promised that they would not rehire any of the boycotting workers and that strikebreakers would have permanent jobs when the strike and boycott ended. The individual lines also recruited strikebreakers, but the General Managers' Association alone was able to recuit several hundred men per day. Before the strike and boycott ended, nearly twenty-five hundred strikebreakers had been sent to Chicago.

In addition, the managers' group took steps designed to maximize public discontent with the boycotters. The railroads intentionally disrupted their own schedules to irritate the public at the union's expense. The railroads attached Pullman cars to freight trains, suburban carriers, and—most important—mail trains. When workers refused to move the trains because of the Pullmans cars, various shippers, passengers, and simple letter-writers had reason to be angry with the union.

As was the case with the boycotting members of the American Railway Union, the members of the General Managers' Association had reasons for acting that went well beyond the actual Pullman controversy. To be sure, many of the railroads had contracts with the Pullman Company that obligated them to run Pullman cars. Pullman could have sued the railroads for failing to live up to these obligations. But there is no evidence that this was an important concern or a contemplated action. Instead, the managers' association seem to have been primarily concerned with the power of the American Railway Union and with what the union represented, namely, industrywide unionism. The railroads had managed to work in the past with the specialized brotherhoods, and several of the brotherhoods even sided with the General Managers' Association during the boycott. The American Railway Union, by contrast, with its size and unity among workers was a threat to railroad capital and needed to be crushed.

———

In retrospect, it is not surprising that the boycott became violent but rather that the violence was slow to begin. With Debs trying desperately to direct 150,000 American Railway Union members, other unions joining the cause, and wildcat strikes breaking out against individual lines, it would have been impossible to prevent violence. With the General Managers' Association sending out spies, hiring strikebreakers, and rerouting their trains to irritate the public, severe social disorder was certain.

The first hints of trouble came several days into the boycott, when union members and sympathizers stopped a Chicago & Erie train near Hammond, Indiana, a town just across the Illinois line from Chicago. Crowds in Chicago then stopped two express trains on the Illinois Central and Panhandle railroads. And the Illinois Central in turn expressed concern that its property in Cairo in the southern tip of Illinois was about to be sabotaged.

Under Illinois law the governor could call out the state's militia if there was a formal request from the local sheriff. When he received requests from sheriffs in Vermilion and Marion Counties, Governor John P. Altgeld ordered six companies of state militia to Danville and another three to Decatur, all with instructions to quell rioting and clear the way for trains. This seemed, at least temporarily, to calm the waters. In Chicago, Mayor Hopkins expressed confidence that order could be maintained. Trains on the Chicago & Erie, Illinois Central, and Panhandle lines began to move. Everyone breathed a sigh of relief.

But alas, panic did not abate in Washington, D.C. President Grover Cleveland assembled his cabinet to discuss how to address the situation in Chicago and elsewhere. Several leading members of the cabinet were cool to the idea of committing federal troops, in part for fear of their ineffectiveness and also in part to avoid embarrassing Mayor Hopkins and Governor Altgeld, both of whom were prominent and powerful in Cleveland's Democratic Party. General Nelson A. Miles, commander of the military department that included Chicago, also advised against the use of federal troops, fearing that the disorder "was very much more deeply rooted, more threatening and far-reaching than anything that had occurred before."

When he realized that the decision had been made to commit troops, Miles was outraged. He asked the president whether the troops should be ordered to fire on strikers and their supporters. Cleveland replied angrily that Miles was "to be the judge on questions of that kind." Cleveland also said, "If it takes every dollar in the Treasury and every soldier in the United States Army to deliver a postal card in Chicago, that postal card shall be delivered."

Central in the decision to commit federal troops was Attorney General Richard Olney. Given his background, Olney was hardly the person one might turn to for a neutral, evenhanded reaction to the strike and boycott. A graduate of both Brown University and the Harvard Law School, Olney had practiced with former congressman and Massachusetts Supreme Court justice Benjamin F. Thomas in Boston. He married Thomas's daughter Agnes and took over Thomas's practice when Thomas died. Olney's most important and lucrative clients were railroads. On at least two occasions he declined apppointment to the Massachusetts Supreme Court, preferring instead to represent railroads before the courts and commissions of New England.

Olney's specialty was not railroad labor squabbles but rather railroad management, merger, and consolidation. He helped transform the Boston & Maine Railroad from a small Boston-to-Portland line into a system that controlled all major railroad traffic north of Boston. He was also the attorney for or a director of the Chicago, Burlington and Quincy; the Atchison, Topeka & Santa Fe; and smaller New England lines such as the Worcester, Nashua and Rochester and the Boston, Revere Beach and Lynn. The Chicago, Burlington and Quincy, incidentally, was the very same line that had broken a strike in 1888 in ways that helped turn Debs from the brotherhoods to industrial unionism. Being a railroad lawyer served Olney extremely well, as his mansion with an elevator on Boston's prestigious Commonwealth Avenue indicated. Olney had before accepting appointment as attorney general sought assurances from President Cleveland that he could continue his private practice while serving in the cabinet. And indeed, Olney continued to receive substantial retainers from several railroads after he moved to Washington, D.C.

Olney's railroad background gave him special standing in the cabinet's discussion of the strike and boycott, and Olney unambiguously advised strong military action. Some have noted how irritated Olney had grown when the ongoing labor unrest threatened his plan to summer on Cape Cod, something to which he had annually treated himself for twenty years. He grumbled about this to Miss A. M. Straw, his loyal secretary and book-keeper. Things were not helped by the hot, humid weather that settled into place in Washington, D.C., in late June and early July and made more difficult Olney's daily tennis matches with his friend Theodore Roosevelt.

More irritating to Olney than disrupted summer plans and unpleasant Washington weather, according to Olney's leading biographer, was the way the boycott affected two of Olney's major clients, the Burlington and Santa Fe railroads, and the interests of several close business associates—Charles Murray Forbes, Charles E. Perkins, Benjamin P. Cheney, and George Pullman himself. In addition, Olney thought that Governor Altgeld, who had pardoned the surviving Haymarket defendants, and Mayor Hopkins, a strike sympathizer from the start, could not be trusted. Olney decreed to one and all, "We have been brought to the ragged edge of anarchy, and it is time to see whether the law is sufficiently strong to prevent this condition of affairs."

Cleveland first put on alert the federal troops at Fort Sheridan, just to the north of Chicago. Then on July 3 Cleveland ordered them into town. They arrived just after midnight on July 4. Chicago at this point was relatively calm. The strike and boycott had greatly hindered rail traffic and led to isolated acts of sabotage, but there had been no large-scale rioting.

Governor Altgeld learned of the order for federal troops only when they arrived in Chicago. He was outraged, and a pungent exchange of telegrams between Altgeld and President Cleveland ensued, with all of Altgeld's telegrams being lengthy and impassioned and Cleveland's short and abrupt. "Waiving all questions of courtesy," Altgeld said, "the state of Illinois is not only able to take care of itself, but it stands ready to furnish the Federal government any assistance it may need elsewhere." The railroads, Altgeld told the president, were not paralyzed because of obstructions and protests but rather because men were unwilling to work on them. Troubles were local, and little violence had occurred. "I protest," Altgeld said with a huff, "against this uncalled for reflection upon our people, and again ask the immediate withdrawal of these troops." In his responses, Cleveland cited his power under the Constitution, requests from postal authorities, and "proof that conspiracies existed against commerce between the States." When Altgeld continued to complain, Cleveland reiterated his belief that he had not transcended his authority. "It seems to me in this hour of danger and public distress," he said in his final telegram, "discussion may well give way to active efforts on the part of all in authority to restore obedience to law and to protect life and property."

General Miles, who actually had been in Washington, D.C., for the cabinet deliberations, arrived in Chicago around noon on July 4 to take command. His headquarters, quite conveniently for some, were in the Pullman Building, and he also established a tent encampment on the Chicago lakefront, not far from the building. After meeting with local advisors, Miles decided suburban Blue Island and the stockyards were especially volatile and dispatched troops to both spots.

Throughout the military intervention, Miles met regularly with John Egan, who in turn kept the General Managers' Association informed of developments. Although Miles had opposed committing federal troops in the first place, he was nevertheless eager to end the strike and disorder. The white ribbons worn by the strikers and their supporters genuinely irked him. He hired men to spy on union meetings, and he told the troops to fire on rioters as needed. Miles considered Debs a would-be dictator. The situation, in Miles's opinion, pitted the forces of lawlessness against civilization. He compared it to Paris in 1791. "Men must take sides," he said, "either for anarchy, secret conclaves, unwritten law, mob violence, and universal chaos under the red or white flag of socialism on the one hand; or on the side of established government."

Pullman remained out of town and did not witness the arrival of the federal troops, but the troops literally gave Debs a rude awakening. He realized that the federal troops had arrived when, on the morning of Independence Day, he awoke, walked to his hotel window, and saw a squad of troops taking up their position immediately outside. He called his brother and trusted advisor Theodore from bed and pointed out the window. "Those fellers aren't militiamen," Debs shouted. "They're regulars. Do you get that? Cleveland has sent the troops in."

Nervous about his own ability to control things and a bit of a Pollyanna, Debs at first welcomed the troops. He thought they might maintain order and allow the strike and boycott to go forward without violence. The thought was as silly as Debs's earlier idea that the railroads would decide to boycott Pullman. Before long, Debs realized that the federal troops were to make sure the trains moved and that this would inevitably undermine the boycott. With Olney advising Cleveland, Egan meeting regularly with Miles, and the troops camping near the Pullman Building, the military was not a neutral peacekeeper but rather a friend of capital.

As in prior and subsequent disturbances in which armed, uniformed troops have been deployed, the presence of soldiers was destabilizing. The soldiers aroused the anger of the American Railway Union and of labor in general. According to union vice president George Howard, a former member of the Union Army, "The very sight of a bluecoat arouses their [workers'] anger; they feel it is another instrument of oppression." In addition, Chicago had many tramps, drifters, and men and women seeking employment. The United States Strike Commission revealed its biases when it commented on the various "hoodlums, women, a low class of foreigners, and recruits from the criminal classes." These people were not members of the American Railway Union, but, in the words of the commission, they were "bent upon plunder and destruction. They gathered whenever opportunity offered for their dastardly work, and, as a rule, broke and melted away when force faced them." Taunting soldiers or throwing a rock at authority was a way to relieve ennui and assert oneself.

Within a day of the first troops reaching Chicago, mobs tipped and set on fire their first railroad cars. The military responded at first not with guns but rather with bayonets and cavalry charges. Success was at best partial, and one mob grew to a reported ten thousand men and young boys. The mob raged through the stockyards and Rock Island property—chanting, throwing bricks, and destroying railroad property. The disturbances of July 5 climaxed with an immense fire of unknown origins in the temporary World's Fair buildings at Jackson Park. The Chicago newspapers rushed extra editions to the streets with headlines such as "Big Riot in the Yards" and "World's Fair in Flames."

Chicagoans feared what the next day would bring, and indeed July 6 saw even more havoc and destruction. A security guard on the Illinois Central shot two rioters, and a mob rose in outrage. Rioters ignited cars with torches, and the flames jumped from row to row of the parked trains. The fire department attempted to put out the fires, but hoses could not reach outlying areas in the yards. In the Panhandle yards in South Chicago at least seven hundred cars were destroyed by a mob numbering roughly six thousand. On July 6 alone, the Managers estimated, railroad property valued at $340,000 dollars had been lost.

No subsequent day equaled July 6 in property loss, but rioting continued for several days, leaving eleven more dead and fifty wounded. Chicago train service came to almost a complete stop. Miles requested and Cleveland ordered reinforcements from Kansas, Michigan, Nebraska, and

New York, bringing federal troops to two thousand. On July 8 the president issued a formal proclamation ordering crowds to disperse and warning that the troops were authorized to act forcefully, that is, shoot if necessary. Even larger numbers of federal marshals, militiamen, police, and private railroad guards were on duty, and though martial law was not declared, Chicago seemed to many a war zone.

The boycott also resulted in violence, rioting, and the use of federal troops outside of Chicago. Indeed, the troubles in other parts of the country were so numerous and extensive as to stymie an especially thorough historian of the 1940s. He wrung his hands and wrote: "In surveying the nation-wide scope of the struggle one becomes bewildered at the multiplicity of incidents and rapidity with which events transpired."

The East was the quietest. As noted, the American Railway Union had a relatively small membership in that region, and, coincidentally, Pullman had his least success leasing and renting cars to eastern lines. Several eastern lines, in fact, were publicly loyal to the Wagner Palace Car Company and the Monarch Sleeping Car Company, two of Pullman's chief rivals. Furthermore, as the General Managers' Association had realized, the East had a large population of unemployed workers who could have served as strikebreakers.

If the East was quiet, the Midwest, Southwest, and West were not. In Hammond, Indiana—Chicago's eastern door—union members and others toppled trains, attacked "scabs," and even seized the local telegraph office. In Spring Valley, Illinois, striking miners joined the boycotters to stop trains, and in Dubuque and Sioux City, Iowa, boycotters spiked switches. In the Cherokee Strip of the Oklahoma Territory, bridges were blown up and trains derailed. In Ogden, Utah, workers took complete control of the railroad yards and also set fires in the city itself. In New Mexico trains were stopped, and workers detained passengers and the mails. In the most populated areas of California—from Los Angeles to San Francisco and Oakland to Sacramento—union members and their supporters toppled and seized trains.

From his base in Chicago, Debs continued frantically to wire his locals urging calm, but many of the rioters were not even affiliated with the American Railway Union. They had axes to grind against the railroads, capital, and the economic system in general, and the boycott presented a chance to start grinding. Police and federal marshals attempted to quell the disturbances, and on President Cleveland's order, over sixteen thousand more federal soldiers were mustered from six of the country's eight formal military areas. In addition to the deaths in Chicago, forty died in clashes with federal troops or militiamen in six other states.

———

Never before had the nation seen a strike and boycott of such frightening magnitude. The country's second largest city was convulsed by violence and mayhem and virtually occupied by federal troops. Train traffic from Minnesota to Texas and from Indiana to California stalled and in many areas stopped completely. At the peak of the strike and boycott an estimated quarter of a million workers in twenty-seven states were on strike, disrupting rail traffic, or rioting. *Harper's Weekly* thought the nation was "fighting for its own existence just as truly as in suppressing the great rebellion."

And in the *Harper's* analogy it was clear that the strikers, boycotters, and their sympathizers were the equivalent of the southern rebels of three decades earlier. While at the beginning of the original strike, many Americans were supportive of the union and hostile to Pullman, the boycott and rioting had carried the great majority to the railroad side. Farmers were worried about getting their crops to market. Individuals were concerned about the mails and the availability and price of goods. And even though railroad provocation and the federal troops had on some level prompted rioting and violence, most of the public held the workers responsible for what had transpired.

Ministers preached against the boycott, Congress supported Cleveland's use of federal troops, and the press, both in Chicago and nationally, turned brutally against Debs, the union, and labor. The *Chicago Tribune* led a half dozen Chicago dailies in suggesting an anarchist mob had seized the city by the throat. One of its headlines screamed, "Law Is Trampled On— Riotous Emissaries of Dictator Debs." The *Daily Inter Ocean* decreed, "This is not fight of labor against capital. It is a criminally injudicious attack of certain forces of organized labor upon every other kind of labor and upon all popular interests in common." The *Washington Post* on July 7 featured the headline "Fired by the Mob, Chicago at the Mercy of the Incendiary's Torch," and *Harper's Weekly* characterized the strike and boycott as "blackmail on the largest scale."

George Pullman disappeared at least temporarily from the press coverage, and the General Managers' Association seemed only an abstraction.

By contrast, Debs became the true bête noire. On July 2, the *Chicago Herald* suggested, "Short work should be made of this reckless, ranting, contumacious, impudent braggadocio and law breaker," and the *Daily Inter Ocean* said he was "as much a criminal as are the outlaws who hold up trains in the far west." The *New York Times,* in the type of rhetorical gesture often used for radicals, questioned Debs's health and sanity, saying he had been treated for dipsomania and wondering if his conduct was not "due to the disordered condition of his mind and body, brought about by the liquor habit."

Beyond its headlines, stories, and editorials, the press also brought the visual to bear. The American press reported the strike and boycott with more pictures than ever before used for a single event. The pictures included line sketches, pen and wash ink drawings, engravings from sketches, photographs, and halftone reproductions of photographs. Perhaps the most famous drawings were rendered by prominent artist Frederic Remington. He reprised his earlier renderings of soldiers in the West with a series of renderings of soldiers in Chicago for *Harper's Weekly.* The soldiers, in Remington's mind, halted the advance of a "malodorous crowd of anarchist foreign trash." The "decent people of Chicago" received the troops well, in hopes of keeping "social scum from rising to the top."

Political cartoons added the overt judgments not always obvious in the sketches and photographs. Between July 3 and 5, for example, the *Chicago Tribune* ran a nasty series of front-page cartoons mocking Debs. In the first of the cartoons, Debs appears as a jackass with long ears and hooves wearing a lion's suit and braying at Uncle Sam. At Debs's feet are trampled train cars and a volume titled "LAW." In the second, Debs sheds his lion's suit but dons a crown. He tells two boys Independence Day has been ended. On the floor an American eagle is tied to a spittoon, and on the wall "ARU" has replaced "Union" in a "The Union Forever" sign. In the third cartoon, Uncle Sam strikes back. Using a wand labeled "U.S. Troops," he lights the fuse of a firecracker that appears to be the lawless Debs himself!

Harper's Weekly only had one shot at Debs per week, but it managed to be just as nasty as the *Chicago Tribune.* The *Harper's* cover of July 14 featured a rather jaunty short-sleeved Debs wearing a crown and sitting astride a bridge labeled "Highway of Trade." In the background a passenger depot, freight depot, factory, and grain elevator stood closed, and trains with vegetables, beef, pork, flour, and mail were stalled. One week later, the cover of the same journal featured paraders, including Governor Altgeld, carrying the crowned Debs in a litter, followed by a monstrous menagerie of man-beasts with torches and guns. The drawing was titled "Vanguard of Anarchy."

With sensationalist reporting and imagery run amuck, one could very easily have lost sight of the essential character of the conflict. The *New York Times* deserves credit, at least, for seeing it. The troubling, mushrooming Pullman strike and boycott, the *Times* told readers, was "in reality ... a struggle between the greatest and most important labor organization and the entire railroad capital." Writing somewhat later, Jane Addams, the reformer, sociologist, and founder of the Chicago Hull House settlement, recalled all the confusion induced by the strike and boycott. Many of her fellow workers at Hull House wore white ribbons in solidarity with the strikers, but Addams herself had been unable to reach a dying sister because of interrupted train service. The strike and boycott had revealed "that distinct cleavage of society." "A quick series of events," she thought, "had dispelled the good nature which in happier times envelopes the ugliness of the industrial situation."

CHAPTER 3

The Strike On Trial

In the midst of the strike and even after federal troops had entered the fray, Eugene Debs remained amazingly optimistic. As late as July 24 he told Jean Daniel Debs and Marguerite Bettrich Debs, his elderly parents in Terre Haute, that the switchmen remained loyal to the cause. "We shall whip Pullman and make him settle," Debs said. "Mark it!" Later, Debs would realize that defeat had arrived quickly on his doorstep. And defeat, in his opinion, had been delivered by neither the General Managers' Association nor the United States Army. What stifled him and the American Railway Union were arrests of union officers, legal orders requiring cessation of strike and boycott activities, and the legally authorized ransacking of union headquarters. "The men went back to work, and the ranks were broken," Debs told a federal commission established to investigate the strike, "by the federal courts of the United States."

Just what happened in the courts? The story is almost as complicated as the story of the strike and boycott. In Chicago alone, Debs and the union leaders were subjected to two separate but intertwined legal proceedings, and each proceeding in itself had numerous courtroom hearings and developments. One of the proceedings also resulted in a dramatic appeal in 1895 to the United States Supreme Court.

The combined proceedings might be thought of as the "legal process" working its way to a conclusion, but such a bland characterization fails on at least two counts. First, the representatives of the government were connected in personal and financial ways with railroad capital and, to a lesser extent, with George Pullman. As the "government" proceeded in the federal civil and criminal courts, it almost always looked to the best interests of the railroads. Second, the representatives of the government themselves were connected in ways that are considered improper. In particular, prosecutors and judges worked closely with one another, leaving representatives of Debs and the other defendants at a severe disadvantage. The Pullman case, at least in trial courts, emerges as something other than neutral adjudication under the rule of law—a presumption that reigned in the dominant American ideology of the period. With good reason, the case may be seen as a biased use of law, legal proceedings, and legal institutions for recognizably political purposes.

One of the trial court proceedings in Chicago was in the civil courts, and the other was in the criminal courts. Civil proceedings customarily involve one party suing another and seeking money damages or some other kind of civil remedy. Sometimes when one party sues another in a civil action, the other party returns the favor and seeks in a countersuit a civil remedy of its own. In a criminal proceeding, by contrast, the government, acting through a prosecutor, seeks to convict one or more parties of a crime. If convicted, the defendant is subjected to criminal penalties, most commonly but not exclusively imprisonment. In the Pullman case, the civil and criminal proceedings took place in the same general time frame; neither came first nor even concluded before the other. However, it will perhaps be useful to discuss the civil and criminal proceedings independently of one another.

At the heart of the civil proceeding was an injunction and a slightly later allegation that Debs, other union leaders, and various strikers and boycotters had violated the injunction. Known in English law from as early as the fourteenth century, an injunction is an order from a judicial officer directing somebody either to do or not to do something. Injunctions are not final decisions in a legal controversy. Judges issue them not on the legal merits of an underlying claim but rather to prevent irreparable harm while things are being sorted out. Hence, a judge may enjoin a person from dumping waste into a pond until ownership of the pond is determined. Or a judge might order a party to let a neighbor use a path until rights to the use of the path are clarified.

The American court system drew heavily on its English origins, and from the beginning of the Republic state and federal judges heard petitions for and sometimes granted injunctions. The judges also heard other kinds of requests and decided matters in different ways, but judges customarily heard injunction requests while sitting in what is called "equity jurisdiction." Article III of the United States Constitution gave federal judges the power to hear cases in "law and equity," and in essence the federal judges in Chicago while sitting in equity issued an injunction telling Debs and his colleagues to stop certain of their strike and boycott activities.

The chief engineers of the successful attempt to obtain an injunction were United States Attorney General Richard Olney and his handpicked assistant Edwin Walker. The latter was a prominent senior railroad lawyer, having represented at least one railroad, and sometimes more than one, for the preceding thirty-five years. Walker was also a law partner of a member of the General Managers' Association legal committee. Olney liked Walker, thought he had the right moral and political principles, and asked him to serve as special assistant United States attorney for the government in the Chicago proceedings against Debs and the union.

Nobody missed the obvious bias of this appointment. The young Chicago attorney Clarence Darrow, himself a railroad lawyer, was incensed by the appointment, a reaction that would contribute shortly to a major political and career shift on Darrow's part. Even in the inner circles of railroad ownership and management, questions surfaced about the Walker appointment. To some extent, the disagreement concerned who could best serve the railroads' interests. Some questioned Walker's ability and warned about his health. Additionally, some wondered about the appearance such an appointment would leave. Did it make the government's preferences a bit too obvious?

Olney, in any case, was not one to reconsider his decisions and held firm regarding the Walker appointment. With Olney and Walker calling the shots, standing Chicago United States Attorney Thomas M. Milchrist on July 2, 1894, filed a so-called bill in equity with Chicago judges Peter S. Grosscup and William A. Woods. The two judges sat, respectively, in Chicago's United States District Court and United States Circuit Court—both trial courts in the federal system of the 1890s. Until eliminated by the Judiciary Act of 1911, the circuit court was the more prestigious of the two, but as the Chicago proceeding suggested, the district and circuit courts could in special cases be combined, leaving not one but two judges presiding.

The bill in equity was in essence a petition summarizing the harm allegedly being done to the railroads and commerce, and it went on to request that an injunction be issued. No one doubted that Judges Grosscup and Woods would be receptive to the request. Grosscup's brother was another railroad lawyer, working for the Northern Pacific Railroad. And only a month earlier Grosscup himself had given a much publicized Decoration Day address excoriating labor federations as a menace to civilization. The American worker, Grosscup had said, "has effectively sunk his will into the general will of his trade and has cast away for organization all the advantages and inspiration of independent individuality." Grosscup also feared the emergence of one big union—"a still deeper tyranny" in his terms. "Sunken individuality," in his opinion, would "destroy the basis on which business in the long run can be successful and debase the man."

Grosscup was careful in his address to make clear he was speaking as a citizen rather than as a judge, that he was not purporting to interpret existing laws. But the prominent railroad lawyers and United States Attorney Milchrist, all of whom the *Daily Inter Ocean* said adjourned from the speech to a banquet honoring Grosscup at Union Hall, could not have missed the ramifications of the judge's philosophy for specific cases. The judge was on the side of capital.

Prior to the formal filing of the bill in equity, Judges Grosscup and Woods actually worked with Walker and Milchrist to shape and perfect it. On the same day as the filing the judges then issued the injunction itself and also ordered federal marshals to distribute ten thousand copies of it along the railroad lines. The injunction, with good reason, struck many as "omnibus," that is, relating to or providing for many things at once. It ordered the union to desist and refrain from interfering with, hindering, obstructing, or stopping any of the involved railroads and also from interfering with any trains carrying the United States mail. Union officials, according to the injunction, were also to stop compelling or inducing any railroad workers to cease work. The officials were not by threat or intimidation to prevent anyone from beginning to work for the railroads. The injunction, in other words, addressed the movement of rail traffic, people who worked for the railroads, and people who might start working for the railroads in the midst of the strike. The injunction did not simply order the strike and boycott to end, but in the opinion of some it might just as well have said that.

Even some conservative members of the legal profession wondered about the expansiveness of all this. At the August 1894 meeting of the American Bar Association, for example, Charles Chaflin Allen of St. Louis gave a speech questioning the propriety of the injunction. He particularly challenged the language in the injunction concerning "ten thousand strikers and all the world besides," and he also did not like the way the injunction had been served. In Chicago, at least, the injunction had been published in the local newspapers before actually being served on Debs and his colleagues. Debs, literally, read of the injunction before formally receiving it. Then, to make things even worse in Allen's opinion, "service" of the injunction included its unpredictable posting on the sides of railroad cars.

For his own part, Debs had grasped the importance of federal troops arriving in Chicago a few days after the issuance of the injunction, but he may not have understood the significance of the actual injunction. Debs was largely self-educated and at this point in his life still unsophisticated about the twists and turns of the law. He was also such an incredibly optimistic man that he sometimes flirted with naivete. Upon receiving the service of the injunction, he consulted with William W. Erwin, the hardworking lawyer for the union, and Erwin told him simply to carry on while attempting to restrain violence. Debs followed the advice but said on July 4, two days after the issuance of the injunction, "I cannot see the necessity for serving an injunction on me commanding me not to do that which the statutes of the state also require me not to do."

Others, both then and now, could see what Debs was missing and what was so noteworthy about the omnibus injunction. It barred so much and prevented so many things that if followed, it would disable the union. Perhaps one could understandably enjoin physical abuse of "scabs" or the burning of railroad cars, but how about picketing and encouraging workers to leave the job? How about telling strike and boycott leaders to fight on? All of these were enjoined as well. The *Chicago Tribune* observed on the very day the injunction was issued that it was "so broad and sweeping that interference with the railroads, even of the remotest kind, will be made practically impossible."

Debs had reason to learn an important legal lesson two weeks after the issuance of the injunction when lawyers for the railroads and the federal government returned to court to argue that Debs, union vice president George W. Howard, union secretary Sylvester Keliher, and union newsletter editor Lewis W. Rogers were in contempt of court for failing to abide by the injunction. At this July 17 hearing, George R. Peck, chair of the General Managers' Association legal committee and attorney for the Santa Fe Railroad, made the argument for the railroads. The Santa Fe itself was in a federal receivership because of its financial difficulties, and under the law of the time this gave Peck standing to make his pitch. Walker and Milchrist, meanwhile, appeared as lawyers for the government, but given

{ *The Pullman Case* }

shared presentations and overlapping loyalties, it was difficult to tell where railroad arguments ended and government arguments began.

The argument in both petitions was, essentially, that Debs and the others had violated the injunction. In particular, the petitioners pointed to a stack of telegrams sent from Chicago to union leaders in other parts of the country. Signed "Eugene V. Debs," "E. V. Debs," or simply "Debs," the telegrams are a fascinating indicator of the attitudes and strategies of the union leadership in the midst of the nation's largest struggle between capital and labor. Some of the telegrams went in identical form to multiple recipients, while others were individualized. Some were only a sentence or two in length, while others reached nine or ten sentences. In many Debs simply reports on strike developments, naming railroads and states that had been tied up. Often, Debs is a cheerleader, urging the men to have hope and to fight on. "We are gaining grandly everywhere. Strike now reaches eastern Ohio. We will simply win," Debs wired C. S. McAuliff in Milwaukee. "Don't get scared by troops or otherwise. Stand pat," Debs urged O. L. Vincent in Clinton, Iowa. "Not men enough in the world to fill vacancies and more occurring hourly."

Frequently the telegrams warn against believing newspaper accounts or rumors, especially if the latter come from "corporation lickspitters." Also present is a late-Victorian emphasis on "manhood" or "true manhood." The strikers and boycotters, Debs thought, should be true to and rely on their masculinity. "Stand erect," Debs pleaded. "Proclaim your manhood." The overall struggle, Debs was certain, pitted "labor" against "capital." "The lines are sharply drawn," Debs wired James Curry in Ft. Wayne. "All who work are assisting capital defeat labor." Debs told M. King in Glenn's Ferry, Idaho, that a particularly menacing federal marshal was "simply assisting capital to enslave his brother."

To what extent did the telegrams in fact constitute a violation of the injunction? They included no specific directions to start fires or destroy railroad cars. Putting aside one joking telegram to a man named Courthead in South Butte, Montana, that reported, "Potatoes and ice are out of sight. Save your money and buy a gun," the telegrams are completely non-violent. Indeed, in many of the telegrams Debs says explicitly, "Commit no violence." However, the telegrams did urge union leaders to get the men to strike and boycott. "Tie up the roads that insist on handling boycotted cars," Debs wired A. P. Merriman in Memphis. "Every true man must quit now and remain out until the fight is won," Debs said in an identical wire to leaders in various parts of the country. Railroad and government lawyers argued that instructions of this sort led to an interference with interstate commerce and in other ways violated the injunction.

Debs and his overmatched legal counsel tried to point out that the union leadership had never seized any railroad property or engaged in violence and were therefore not in contempt. But the tight and friendly connections between the railroads and the government attorneys and the comparably tight and friendly connections between the government attorneys and judges made the union arguments futile. After listening to a reading of some of the telegrams, Judge William H. Seaman, the only federal judge in town when the contempt citation was sought, decreed that he had heard enough. He did not actually find Debs, Howard, Keliher, and Rogers in contempt, but he did order a body attachment, that is, the temporary holding of the defendants. Seaman also set bail at three thousand dollars each and set another hearing for July 23.

Federal marshals did not have to hunt down the union leaders as if they were fugitives. All surrendered on the same afternoon the attachment order issued. Then, to the surprise of many, the defendants waived bail and were as a result hustled off to jail. The befuddled Walker speculated in a telegram to Olney that the waiver of bail was either a ploy to win sympathy for the union cause or an indication that union leadership needed a respite from the struggle.

As incomprehensible as it might have been to Walker, the union leaders understood their refusal to be released on bail as a matter of principle. Lewis Rogers, the union's chief journalist, said the large amount (three thousand dollars) was not the key. "If it was $2, I'd go to jail. This is a mighty test between labor and capital, and we will fight it to the finish." "The poor striker who is arrested would be thrown in jail," Debs said. "We are no better than he." The goal, Debs was certain, was "to test the question as to whether men can be sent to jail without trial for organizing against capital."

Debs also wrote on July 24 to Henry Demarest Lloyd, the scholarly critic whose attack on Standard Oil in *Wealth against Nations* had garnered much attention. He and the others, Debs reported to Lloyd, had acted "in obedience to the dictates of our consciences" and would as a result "accept with philosophic composure any penalties, however severe, the courts may see fit to impose." Debs hoped the strike and legal proceedings involving the injunction were calling the attention of the country to the flagrant abuses of corporate power of which working people have so long been the patient and uncomplaining victims. I am inclined to be optimistic and do not hesitate to believe that all these things are making for the emancipation and redemption of men from the thralldom that has so long been theirs in slavery and degradation.

Debs' principled conduct led to a specific place: the Cook County Jail in the heart of downtown Chicago. Like other urban jails in major cities of the 1890s, the Cook County Jail, with its massive granite walls and narrow windows, was designed to threaten potential wrongdoers as much as it was to house actual ones. The corridors and cells were filthy with tobacco spit, body wastes, and moldy growths. Debs' own cell housed five other men, with bunks stacked three high against the two major walls. The mattresses were filled with bugs, and the inmates scratched the bug bites until they bled. Rats also ranged through the jail, and on one occasion Debs asked to borrow a guard's fox terrier in order to counterattack the rodents. Unfortunately, the rats frightened the dog more the dog frightened the rats. With the dog whimpering and howling in fright, the guard removed it from the cell for its own protection.

Other proceedings and imprisonments followed for Debs in the course of his long, activist life, but the experiences in the Cook County Jail always stayed with him. Later, in his famous essay about why he had become a socialist, he recalled the way jailers had treated him. His cell, not coincidentally, overlooked the very place where just a few years earlier the Haymarket anarchists had been hanged. A jailer also showed Debs the bloodstained rope used in the most recent execution and described the execution "in minutest detail." Debs may not until then have understood the way he could be seen as a political prisoner, but the point seemed finally to register on him.

While battling the injunction and the yet to be discussed simultaneous criminal prosecution, Eugene Debs realized it would be prudent to recruit more lawyers for his side. Up until the imprisonment, Debs and the union had relied primarily on their regular attorney, William W. Erwin of Minneapolis, but with experienced railroad and government counsel moving forward on several fronts, the union needed more help. Union representatives consulted senior Chicago lawyers with labor sympathies, and after these consultations the representatives invited Stephen S. Gregory and Clarence Darrow to work for the union. The latter of course went on to great fame as a defense lawyer for underdogs, but at the time of the invitations Gregory was the more prominent of the two. Forty-five years of age, Gregory was well known in Chicago legal circles for his independence and courage. In most of the subsequent courtroom proceedings, Gregory occupied the defense's first chair. In later years he went on to serve as president of the Chicago, Illinois, and American Bar Associations. Gregory, in other words, accomplished what many lawyers dream of but few achieve: He was true to his principles and politics, representing clients he took to be disadvantaged, but he also built a lucrative and prestigious practice.

Less well known than Gregory and eight years his junior, Darrow anguished over the invitation to work for Debs and the union. Unbelievable as it may seem in retrospect, Darrow actually worked at the time of the strike for the Chicago & Northwestern Railroad. The strikers, he thought, were no better than their employers and were "often selfish and unreasonable." But he found distasteful the unequal distribution of wealth between labor and capital and professed to sympathize "with almost all efforts to get higher wages and to improve the general conditions for the masses."

An earlier moment of truth had come for Darrow when he was named to the General Managers' Association legal committee. Could he really work for the railroads *against* labor? Darrow went to the president of the Chicago & Northwestern to discuss his possible resignation, but the president talked him out of it, promising to relieve Darrow from the committee assignment and to give him less troubling work. However, Darrow's conscience kept pinching and pinching, and after the imprisonment of Debs, Howard, Keliher, and Rogers, Darrow again met with his railroad superiors. "I knew that it would take all my time for a long period, with no compensation," Darrow said, "but I was on their side, and when I saw poor men giving up their jobs for a cause, I could find no sufficient excuse, except my selfish interest for refusing." Never one to miss an angle, though, Darrow contracted with the Chicago & Northwestern at half of his previous salary for work on matters unrelated to the strike. This arrangement ironically helped subsidize his efforts on behalf of Debs and the union leadership, and Darrow's part-time representation of the Chicago & Northwestern continued for several years after the Pullman case.

Gregory and Darrow participated in several minor hearings involving the injunction in late July, but then the judges formally continued the civil proceedings in the case until the fall. Walker had become ill and had to be accommodated, and the summer heat had become unbearable. Only in September, with Walker up and running again and with the Windy City's most pleasant month lifting the citizens' spirits, did the new defense team have a full opportunity to argue that the injunction and a contempt citation were improper.

The September hearings took place in the federal circuit court in the Monadnock Building with Judge Woods presiding. The gallery, the *Daily News* reported, overflowed, and fifty people were left standing. Still others tried to "climb over each other at the door." Gregory began by asking for a jury trial. "A trial by jury," Gregory argued, "is guaranteed by the Constitution to determine whether our clients are guilty of a misdemeanor." The point was largely rhetorical, and Judge Woods denied the request even before hearing a response from Walker and United States Attorney Milchrist. The proceeding at hand, Woods reminded Gregory, was not a criminal proceeding, and as a result no right to trial by jury existed.

The government lawyers then began proving that Debs and the union had been in contempt. Over the next few weeks they called various witnesses, most of whom were men who worked for the railroads and were prepared to testify that union officials had urged them to strike and boycott. One witness, a Mr. Brennbeck of the Union Rendering Company, told how because of the strike and boycott he could not live up to his contract to remove dead animals from the Panhandle yards. Mrs. Leland Stanford, wife of the California millionaire and railroad baron, stated by affidavit that the strike and boycott had prevented her own private train from reaching home but that Eugene Debs himself had asked the men to let the train go through.

Once again, the government attorneys introduced the notorious telegrams—nine thousand in all—as evidence, and E. M. Mulford, the manager of the Western Union office in Chicago, reluctantly took the stand. He sat with a foot-and-a-half stack of telegrams in front of him and frustrated one and all by meticulously and slowly searching through the stack for individual items. The American Railway Union, Mulford testified, incurred telegram charges of six thousand dollars for the period between June 26, the day the boycott began, and July 17, the day Debs and his colleagues went to jail.

Walker acknowledged privately that the union leadership had itself neither engaged in violence nor stopped a single train, but he was nevertheless certain that the leadership had violated the omnibus injunction. Walker assured his nervous boss, Attorney General Olney, that this argument—and, by extension, the railroads and the federal government—would prevail.

Defense lawyers responded to Walker's presentation of arguments with an unanticipated move. They called no witnesses and introduced no evidence of their own. One reason for this move was the impending criminal conspiracy trial, which was unfolding simultaneously in 1894. As readers a century later may have noted with reference to proceedings against O. J. Simpson or President Clinton, civil and criminal proceedings may draw from and influence one another. By declining to use witnesses and evidence in the September proceedings regarding the injunction and its alleged violation, Gregory and Darrow were hoping to preserve witnesses and evidence for the impending criminal trial. While the hearings regarding contempt were before federal judges, who had already revealed their sympathy for capital and government, the criminal trial would have not only a federal judge but also a jury. This jury, Gregory and Darrow hoped, would show some sympathy for labor and the union.

The September proceedings concluded with oral arguments. Arguing for the government, Milchrist was close to venomous. "I have never known four more dastardly criminals coming into a court of justice than these men," he said.

> I venture to predict—but I hope my prediction will not come true—that thousands of women and children will cry for bread this winter on account of the actions of the directors of the American Railway Union. These men claim to be champions of liberty. Champions of liberty indeed! These men who have set themselves up as champions of liberty have brought misery and bondage upon thousands of homes, and had it not been for the firmness and patriotism of the President of the United States the results of their actions would have been far more serious.

Then, echoing the sentiments of Pullman and his executives during the attempted negotiations at the beginning of the strike, Milchrist insisted, "The American wage-workers should be left to their own judgment in their disputes with their employers and should not be dictated to by professional agitators and street loafers."

Representing some of the "professional agitators" Milchrist presumably had in mind, Darrow was ready to counter. He pointed out that Milchrist liked to say in courtroom arguments that defendants were guilty of especially heinous offenses. Debs and his colleagues were hardly the first defendants so characterized. "There are various kinds of cowards," Darrow said in open court. "It was not brave for this man Milchrist to stand in court where accident has placed him and heap vituperation on these men who cannot reply." Milchrist bristled and tried to interrupt Darrow, but, prefiguring the courtroom presence for which he would be famous in later years, Darrow controlled the stage, at least for the time being. He argued that every man had a right to decide whether to strike and that the union leadership and members were exercising that right.

The *Chicago Herald* reported that Darrow's argument had led Milchrist to "turn red in the face," but the dramatic courtroom exchange had little apparent impact on Judge Woods. The case, he thought, could be the biggest stepping-stone of his career. He felt that with the spotlight shining on him he should take his time and write a dandy of a final opinion. Walker and especially Olney absolutely fumed over the resulting delays.

Only on December 14, more than three months after the start of the September hearings, did Woods formally rule in the case. According to the *Daily News,* he walked into the courtroom wearing his best "black silk gown" and began reading from "a voluminous typewritten affair." "Edwin Walker rested his head upon his hand and listened intently to the reading of the opinion." And he listened and listened. Judge Woods was a full hour into his reading before it became clear to the assembled that Debs, Howard, Keliher, Rogers, and three other men who had been named in the interim were in contempt.

"The right of men to strike peaceably, and the right to advise a peaceable strike, which the law does not presume to be impossible, is not questioned," Woods said. "But if men enter into a conspiracy to any lawful thing, and in order to accomplish this purpose advise workmen to go upon a strike, knowing that violence and wrong will be the probable outcome, neither on law nor on morals can they escape responsibility." Take note, Woods said, that some of the union's supporters "stopped at no means between drawing of a coupling pin and the undermining of a bridge, whereby men should be buried to death." "Much has been made," Woods added,

> of the wrongs on the workmen at Pullman, of an alliance between the Pullman Company and the general managers to depress wages and generally of corporate oppression and arrogance. But it is evident that these things, whatever the facts might have been proved or imagined

to be, could furnish neither justification nor palliation for giving up a city to disorder and for paralyzing the industries and commerce of the country.

Woods went on in his lengthy opinion to discuss the bases of the court's jurisdiction in the matter, an issue that would be hotly debated in a later appeal to the United States Supreme Court. The key, Woods thought, was the Sherman Anti-Trust Act. Introduced by Senator John Sherman of Ohio and passed by the Congress in 1890, the act had made illegal all contracts, combinations, and trusts in restraint of trade. In this legislation Congress had responded to public complaints but also attempted to preempt the issue, to keep state legislatures from acting in a similar vein. Few if any of the members of Congress who had voted for the act contemplated the way it might be used against workers and their unions. But that did not mean such application was inappropriate. In its four short years of existence, Woods thought, the Sherman Anti-Trust Act had been expanded. It may originally have been directed toward corporations and trusts, but as of 1894 it clearly applied to other combinations and conspiracies that restrained trade. The refusal to move Pullman cars and the resulting interference with interstate commerce was an example. Due to the act, the Chicago federal circuit court could and did properly issue an injunction, and if the parties did not abide, the circuit court could and did properly cite them for contempt.

By the time of Woods's ruling, Debs and his colleagues had abandoned their earlier expressions of principle and posted bail. A few weeks in jail awaiting a decision was one thing; six months was another. But now, the union leaders faced another imprisonment. Debs received a six-month sentence, and the others received three months. Woods sent them not to the Cook County Jail but rather to the McHenry County Jail in nearby Woodstock, Illinois. All arrived in early January 1895. Debs wrote immediately to his parents, saying, "Would you believe it? The sheriff Mr. Eckert is an Alsacian and a noble man. The daughters treat me with the greatest kindness." Always the optimist, Debs remained as well the loving son: "My disgrace is doing much to arouse public conscience. No disgrace attaches to the family. You need not blush."

While the civil proceeding growing out of the strike and boycott wound its way toward Woodstock, the criminal proceeding, the second major variety of the legal action against the defendants, simultaneously followed its own path. From the very beginning of his appointment as special assistant United States attorney, Edwin Walker had wanted to proceed in both the civil and criminal courts. Thomas Milchrist initially opposed the two-barreled legal attack, fearing that it would be difficult to succeed in both legal forums. But Walker thought just having two lines of legal attack would keep Debs and the union lawyers so busy that the strike and boycott would collapse. Attorney General Richard Olney sided with Walker, and once Olney's preferences became known, criminal proceedings were initiated to parallel the civil ones.

Of the two approaches, a criminal prosecution of striking labor leaders or unions was the more conventional. During most of the nineteenth century, the primary legal strategy for employers and government officials anxious to end labor actions and to discipline and control unruly workers had been a criminal prosecution. A strike or even the formation of a union could be understood as a criminal "conspiracy." Only in the 1890s did prosecutions of this sort once and for all give way to injunctions issued in the civil courts. Perched as it was in a period during which American laws and legal procedures were changing rapidly, the Pullman controversy included both the conventional criminal prosecution and the use of a civil injunction.

The criminal proceedings began with considerations by a grand jury of charges that a criminal conspiracy was afoot. The grand jury as an institution dates from as early as twelfth-century England, and during the first several centuries of its existence it was largely a body of respected local citizens who attempted to judge the appropriateness of bringing formal criminal charges against someone. These grand jurors knew local personalities and events, and the grand jury itself therefore guarded against manipulative and biased inclinations to prosecute on the part of the Crown. The traditional grand jury's assignment, in essence, was to decide whether a formal charge should be made against one or more defendants. This was not a conviction but rather an accusation. The defendant still had to be tried and convicted in a subsequent trial before any criminal penalties could be meted out.

In contemporary America, the grand jury has evolved into much more of a tool for prosecutors in the state or local courts. Prosecutors present evidence to the dozen or more grand jurors and ask them to decide whether there is probable cause to indict, that is, to go forward with a criminal prosecution. Formal rules of evidence and cross-examinations by lawyers for potential defendants are not anticipated. Since "probable cause" is a much less demanding standard than what is required to convict someone at a trial, some wags have said that in the contemporary setting any prosecutor could, if he or she wanted, convince a grand jury to indict just about anyone.

In Chicago in the 1890s, the federal grand jury stood poised somewhere between its community-defined origins and its contemporary utilization as a prosecutorial tool. On July 6, 1894, Walker told the always overseeing Olney that he had enough material for an effective presentation to the grand jury and that he was certain the grand jury would vote to indict. "We shall be able to show that this conspiracy has extended over the entire northwest," Walker said, "as well as the Pacific coast, and also east through Michigan, Indiana and Ohio." The result of the forthcoming indictment, trial, and conviction of the union leaders, Walker was sure, "will be so serious that a general strike upon any railroad will not again occur for a series of years."

While Walker boasted, members of the General Managers' Association groused. Less familiar with the legal process than Walker, Milchrist, and Olney, the managers' group wanted Debs behind bars as soon as possible. Debs was in their minds a serious and despicable criminal. Why not just arrest him? The president of the Chicago, Milwaukee and St. Paul Railroad complained to Walker, and in one of many episodes illustrating the cooperation of railroad capital and government, Walker scheduled a meeting with the managers' association's legal committee in hopes of quieting the discontent. At the meeting he assured the assembled that he was moving forward forcefully, that a criminal indictment was forthcoming, and that Debs and the other troublemakers would soon receive their just deserts.

When the grand jury met on July 10, it proved Walker right at least with regard to the indictment, that is, the accusation in writing that a crime had been committed. The jurors, surprisingly enough, did not hail from the city of Chicago but rather from surrounding areas. In the city itself many workers and even the mayor himself were sympathetic to the union cause, but rural citizens were perhaps concerned with the impact the strike and especially the boycott would have on the transportation of crops and livestock. Judge Grosscup welcomed the countrified jury and greased the wheels for the prosecution by instructing the jurors that any plan by two or more individuals to stop trains could be a conspiracy and therefore merit prosecution. The alleged conspirators did not have to know all the parts of the plan or even all the planners. The conspirators needed only to know the illegal purpose of the plan and be willing to effectuate this purpose. Grosscup then left the room, allowing the jurors to hear evidence in his absence.

The chief evidence before the grand jury was the ubiquitous pack of telegrams that were also being used in the civil proceedings, and the only witness was the manager of Chicago's Western Union office, who had been subpoenaed to produce copies of the telegrams. He at first objected to giving testimony. The telegrams, he thought, were privileged communication and should not be released without the senders' permission. Grosscup thought such resistance was ridiculous. He threatened the manager with prison, and the manager yielded the telegrams.

The entire grand jury proceeding lasted only two hours, and the jurors then voted hastily to indict the four top officials of the union—Debs himself, Vice President Howard, Secretary Keliher, and Editor Rogers—and also James Merwin. A few minutes later bench warrants went out for the defendants' arrest. As had been the case earlier in proceedings involving contempt in the civil court, no dramatic attempts to escape or police chases followed. Within a day all the defendants were in police custody.

With Debs and his colleagues under lock and key, federal authorities took the opportunity to ransack the union's offices. The marshals exuberantly seized all books and papers and even took the unopened personal mail of Debs and the others. The union headquarters, Debs said, had been "sacked, torn out and nailed up by the 'lawful' authorities of the federal government." The raid had apparently been ordered by Milchrist in ostensible conjunction with the grand jury indictment and subsequent arrests, but it left many upset. Judge Grosscup quickly ordered the return of all mail and private papers. He also summoned Milchrist into open court and reminded him that even though the defendants had been charged with a serious crime, they still had constitutional rights. While the General Managers' Association and Milchrist were pleased to see Debs arrested and perhaps delighted as well by the ransacking of the offices, Grosscup, at least, seemed to realize that the ideological effectiveness of the legal process depended on maintaining at least the veneer of neutrality and propriety. Law could not appear to be the arbiter of social controversy when too fully and obviously aligned with one side in a controversy.

Olney realized as well that law must appear neutral if citizens are to believe in it, and he seemed to think that not Milchrist but rather Walker had been behind the overly eager police raid. Olney's impressions created tension in his relationship with Walker, the man he had chosen and supported as a special prosecutor. "The government," Olney huffed from his base in the nation's capital, "is too strong and its cause too righteous to warrant or require anything of that nature." Walker resented the statement and returned fire: "In this matter Milchrist and I acted in harmony. It is not the time, in my opinion, to make public apologies to any officer of the American Railway Union." Walker was also angry that Olney had expressed his concerns not in private but to the press, thereby subjecting Walker to public censure.

Disagreements among members of the prosecution team had to be put aside quickly because once the indictment had been made, the prosecutors had to begin preparing for the criminal trial itself. The previously discussed civil proceedings involving the injunction and contempt for violation of the injunction were simultaneously moving forward, but with an eye to just the criminal prosecution, Milchrist, Walker, and their assistants began taking depositions and collecting evidence. Many observers seemed to view this as the more significant branch of the government strategy, if only because the possible criminal penalties were much greater than the penalties for a contempt citation. The possibility that Debs and his colleagues could be punished twice did not amount to "double jeopardy," that is, trying somebody twice for the same charge. The civil and criminal proceedings involved the same defendants, and attorneys often turned to the same evidence. The two branches of the proceedings often were integrated, with the same judges sitting on the bench. But in a technical legal sense, the proceedings were different. The defendants could go to jail as a result of either or both.

After many preliminary hearings and filings, the criminal trial finally began in the federal district court on January 24, 1895—sixteen days after the defendants had begun serving their sentences for contempt in the jail in Woodstock. Judge Grosscup presided, and a dozen additional men had joined the original five indicted men as defendants. Beyond the "bar" separating parties and lawyers from laypeople, the gallery was packed with reporters and spectators. Criminal trials had long had the capacity to capture public attention and crystallize popular sentiments, and the proceeding in Chicago's federal criminal court was no exception. The trial of Debs and his colleagues was a major "event" as the Windy City and the nation launched the new year.

At the very outset, Gregory offered an objection that is certainly understandable to the historian a century later. He suggested that it was inappropriate for Walker to represent the government while continuing to serve as an attorney for the Chicago, Milwaukee and St. Paul Railroad. Perhaps sensing obvious skepticism about his true employer, Walker defensively challenged the allegation that he still worked for the railroad. Judge Grosscup reassured him and ruled that, regardless of Walker's employment, the court could not question Attorney General Olney's choice as special assistant United States attorney. The issue, in other words, was deemed a nonissue.

The trial then began in earnest with an opening statement offered by Milchrist. All the violence and disruption, he asserted, could be credited to the defendants. Debs and the union leaders may not themselves have committed violent acts or physically disrupted train service. The defendants may not have even met as a self-conscious group to discuss specific plans to stop the trains. But criminal conspiracy, Milchrist reminded the jurors, did not require these varieties of conduct.

Darrow responded and in his opening statement cast Milchrist as a "puppet in the hands of the great railroad corporations in this persecution, not prosecution." The infamous telegrams, Darrow asserted, frequently advised strike leaders to avoid violence and lawbreaking. How, Darrow asked, could the lawlessness and disruption be seen as the product of the defendants' conspiracy? Darrow reminded the jurors that a crime required both the intent and an act. The defendants did not intend to disrupt train service and the transport of the mails. They even offered to cut out the Pullman cars so that trains could move on. It was the railroads that effectively stopped the trains and mail deliveries. The plan of the General Managers' Association, Darrow was sure, was "to use the inconvenience of the public and the feeling of sanctity for the mails as a club to defeat the effort that was being made to better the condition of workingmen and women." Darrow continued,

> The evidence will show that all the defendants did was in behalf of the employees of that man whose name is odious wherever men have a drop of blood, Mr. Pullman. No man or newspaper undertook to defend Mr. Pullman except the General Managers' Association, and their defense gives added proof of his infamy.

After the opening statements, both sides presented their evidence and called their witnesses. Perhaps the most striking of the witnesses was Debs himself. The proud son of Terre Haute, who had moved only cautiously and haltingly to a position of labor leadership and militancy, was a thirty-nine-year-old man when he took the stand. He was neither wild-eyed nor strident. Looking a bit like a rising banker with his receding hairline and conservative suit, Debs methodically shared the history of the American Railway Union. He claimed that he was neither a radical nor even a trouble-maker. The strike, he said under oath, was simply a lawful attempt to achieve what was fair.

Debs had been impressive, and George Pullman would have been hard-pressed to match the performance had he even taken the stand at the trial. However, Pullman was unwilling to testify. As had been the case when the strike wore on and turned into a boycott, Pullman kept a low profile. He wanted to avoid the public eye. Judge Grosscup subpoenaed him, but the federal marshal was unable to serve the subpoena. Pullman dodged him and scooted out of Chicago. Only after the jury had been dismissed did he return to town. Represented by this point by Robert Todd Lincoln, son of the assassinated and venerated president, Pullman made a personal call on Judge Grosscup and managed quietly to squelch any suggestion that he had acted improperly. The special treatment, Debs said later, was just one more example of bias. If he had done what Pullman had done, he would have ended up in jail. "There is something wrong in this country," he said, when "the judicial nets are so adjusted to catch minnows and let the whales slip through."

At the trial, meanwhile, the most dramatic development involved the revelation of minutes of General Managers' Association meetings. The union, as noted in the previous chapter, had held open and public meet-ings at the Turner Hall in Kensington, while the managers' group had plot-ted behind closed doors to hire detectives, take names, reroute trains, and build a legal case. Darrow managed to obtain the minutes of the managers' association's meetings and to present them as evidence that the rail-roads were themselves united in a conspiracy to reduce wages, control the union, and prevent the formation of a national labor organization. Who, jurors had reason to wonder, was really up to what?

Before the jurors could make up their mind, the criminal trial ground to a screeching, and for some unwelcome, stop. On February 8, 1895, a juror named John C. Coe was reported to be ill. A physician was sent to visit him in the Clifton and reported that Coe could not be expected to resume his jury service for at least a month. Judge Grosscup also visited Coe in his room and confirmed the seriousness of his condition.

Fearing that a hard-fought victory was about to be snatched from their grasp, Debs and Darrow wondered just how sick the missing juror really was. They proposed that a new juror be appointed to join the remaining eleven. The evidence, they thought, could be read to the newcomer. Judge Grosscup ruled that such replacement was impossible. He discharged the remaining eleven jurors and formally continued the case until May. The prosecution could remount the whole case at that point if it wished, and the next time everyone's health might last. Gregory and Debs were outraged. They thought the case had been won. All but one of the jurors, Darrow claimed, were inclined to acquit the defendants.

———

Proceedings in Chicago's civil and criminal courts against Eugene Debs and his labor colleagues were models for government attorneys in other cities. After the injunction was issued in Chicago on July 2, 1894, similar, and indeed sometimes identical, injunctions were issued in other cities. Often they named the head of the American Railway Union local; if there was not one, they simply named local labor leaders and activists. When Edwin Walker and Thomas Milchrist sought a criminal indictment from the Chicago grand jury, their counterparts in other cities did the same with regard to local labor leaders and activists. Prosecutors outside of Chicago often lacked the resources and evidence available to Walker and Milchrist, but sometimes an indictment in and of itself was enough to quell remaining strike and boycott activity. Given an indictment, arrests could be made, and strike leaders could at least temporarily be incarcerated. Often, union and strike leaders could not post bail. In some cases, the government in effect acknowledged the weakness of its position by later dropping the indictments. But by then the strike and boycott were over.

None of these proceedings in other cities received the national attention the proceedings in Chicago did, and they may not always have been marked by the troubling bias and inside connections so prevalent in Chicago. But in Chicago, from beginning to end the civil and criminal proceedings revealed ties between the railroad capitalists and the government attorneys and their arguments. Olney, Walker, and Milchrist all had substantial connections to the railroads through their own earlier practices. The injunction the attorneys sought and obtained was everything the railroads could have hoped for, and the request for a contempt citation followed quickly in due course. Walker in particular consulted frequently throughout both the civil and criminal proceedings with the General Managers' Association and especially with its legal committee chaired by

George Peck. Did the government ever take a major position not supported and perhaps even cleared in advance with the railroads?

In addition, the prosecutors and the judges worked hand in hand, betraying the notion of an adversary process with a neutral judicial overseer. Judge Woods advised Walker on how to shape the bill in equity and also accommodated Walker's illness. On countless occasions, both Judge Woods and Judge Grosscup ruled on behalf of the government, sometimes even before the government made its full arguments. Overall, the judges were aligned with the prosecutors every bit as much as the prosecutors themselves were aligned with the railroads.

The Pullman case would shortly be appealed to the United States Supreme Court, but at least in the trial courts it stank of collusion. Debs was right in thinking that the federal courts had been instrumental in ending the strike and boycott. He failed only to perceive just exactly how the courts worked with capital and also how the functionaries of the courts worked with one another.

CHAPTER 4

In the Eyes of the United States Supreme Court

Even before commencing their defense of Eugene Debs and the other American Railway Union leaders in the Chicago criminal conspiracy prosecution, Stephen Gregory and Clarence Darrow launched an appeal of the contempt citation for violation of the civil injunction. In Washington, D.C., Attorney General Richard Olney and his assistants were prepared to argue the opposite side. The appellate, as opposed to trial, process culminated on Monday morning, May 27, 1895, when the United States Supreme Court in *In re Debs* unanimously upheld the Chicago federal court's contempt citation.

The Supreme Court at the time included a majority of justices who had earlier in their careers represented one railroad or another, and the justices in general were sympathetic to the arguments and worldview of railroad and government representatives. The Supreme Court's decision, in effect, to side with capital and the government was therefore hardly surprising. At the same time, though, the appellate proceedings were not pocked by the detectable biases and secret arrangements that often made the Chicago courtroom proceedings so troubling. The drama in Washington, D.C., was of a more genuinely legal nature. Political preferences and power notwithstanding, the case played its way out on several legal levels.

The most obvious level of course involved who would win the case, the appellants or the government. In the American legal system, lawyers in an appeal generally do not present new evidence or call new witnesses. They instead are expected to move beyond the "factual" record of the lower court proceedings to more distinctly "legal" questions. However, appellate lawyers do have clients. They still represent appellants and appellees, and it is anticipated that one or the other will come away victorious in an appellate as well as a trial court of law.

On a second level, the appellate process involved what the controlling law and legal principles would be. Laypeople sometimes think that the "law" is clear and fixed, that you can look it up and know it unambiguously. This is rarely true, and it was certainly not the case in a controversy so complex and multifaceted as the Pullman strike and boycott. The arguments on appeal were not simply about whether Debs and his colleagues broke a law or did not. The arguments did not even rest on the same legal concepts and premises. All could, perhaps, begin with the lengthy and long overdue opinion Judge William A. Woods had issued in Chicago upholding the contempt citation, but that was only a starting point. The lawyers on the opposing sides went on to vigorous written and oral argument about how the controversy should be shaped legally. They provided the Supreme Court with a variety of legal frames for making sense of the extended dispute, and the Court's decision in the end constituted a definitive legal rarefaction of epic struggle.

On one final level, the legal drama playing its way out before the United States Supreme Court in 1895 involved not just the search for a final decision and appropriate legal frame but also the definition of law itself. All Supreme Court cases go beyond the specific issues at hand to reflect either explicitly or implicitly on what law as a whole can promise the citizens of the Republic. At many points in the *In re Debs* appellate process and decision the participants offered thoughts about law as a whole. *In re Debs,* in short, involved the philosophy and ideology of law as well as the propriety and meaning of a contempt citation.

Stephen Gregory and Clarence Darrow remained the lead attorneys for Debs and the other American Railway Union officials, but when Gregory and Darrow decided to appeal the case, they realized they needed help. The two attorneys were justifiably confident of their legal skills, but they wanted assistance in the governmental and political arenas. Although in the rail yards, the courts of Chicago, and elsewhere, many workers and even members of the bar had deplored government conduct, governmental and political leaders remained overwhelmingly opposed to the union position. If Gregory and Darrow could attract someone of governmental and political stature to their side, it might enhance their chances before the Supreme Court.

With these thoughts in mind, Gregory and Darrow approached Lyman Trumbull. A senior luminary then in his eighties, Trumbull had been a political and legal rival of Lincoln during the antebellum decades in Illinois. In later years Trumbull served several distinguished terms in the United States Senate. As a member of the Senate Committee on the Judiciary, he had been chiefly responsible for drafting and presenting to the full Senate the Thirteenth Amendment to the United States Constitution, which in a constitutional sense ended slavery. Trumbull left the Senate in 1873 and returned to Illinois. He continued to dabble in politics, but he also resumed an active practice of law, counting William Jennings Bryan among the law clerks who served in his office. Trumbull was one of the founders of the American Bar Association, and he also taught constitutional law at Chicago's Union College of Law. When his class reached the Thirteenth Amendment, Trumbull liked to call special attention to what he considered his greatest accomplishment. "Gentlemen," he would say, "this good right hand wrote this Amendment to the Constitution."

When Gregory and Darrow called on Trumbull for assistance, it constituted a bit of a payback. As noted in the previous chapter, Debs and the American Railway Union officials had earlier looked for additional counsel. They had in the process called on Trumbull, among others, for advice. Trumbull had suggested Gregory and Darrow. They were, he thought, the type of idealistic lawyers who might be willing to take on Pullman, the General Managers' Association, and the federal government. Trumbull, Gregory, and Darrow knew each other well from Chicago legal circles, and Trumbull and Darrow had even for a time occupied offices in the same building at 115 Monroe Street.

Now Gregory and Darrow wanted Trumbull on board, and the latter, increasingly attracted to populist and radical causes in his senior years, agreed. Work at the trial level, Trumbull had concluded accurately, would have been too taxing for his health and stamina. But he could still write an appellate brief and make an oral argument before the United States Supreme Court. Trumbull agreed to provide his services without a fee and asked only for traveling expenses. His mere presence, Gregory and Darrow hoped, would lend a certain dignity and credence to their cause. Trumbull, they might more privately have felt, would be especially influential with United States Supreme Court Chief Justice Melville W. Fuller. Trumbull, after all, had played a major role in securing Fuller's 1888 confirmation as chief justice.

Working quickly, the legal team of Gregory, Darrow, and the newly recruited Trumbull first sought a writ of error, that is, an order from the Supreme Court to the Chicago trial court that a mistake had been made and the judgments should be set aside. When this petition failed, the attorneys turned to the venerable writ of habeas corpus, the writ Sir William Blackstone once called "the most celebrated writ in English law." If amenable, a court through a writ of habeas corpus might rule that somebody should be released from unlawful imprisonment, that somebody should have his liberty restored. A writ of habeas corpus does not mean that a defendant is innocent of the charges; it means rather that he or she has been improperly restrained. The defense lawyers asserted that the contempt citation for violating the omnibus injunction was improper and that, as a result, Debs and the other officers of the American Railway Union should be released from the jail at Woodstock, Illinois.

The defense team presented their petition to Justice John Marshall Harlan of the Supreme Court. Historians have accorded Justice Harlan some special respect because of his appropriately crabby dissent in the infamous 1896 *Plessy v. Ferguson* decision, which in effect upheld southern Jim Crow laws. But in 1895 Harlan was not necessarily the leading light of the Supreme Court. Bill collectors were always on his trail, and Oliver Wendell Holmes described Harlan's mind as "a great vise, the two jaws of which could never be closed." Perhaps most intriguing from a defense perspective, Stephen Gregory counted Harlan's son as his Chicago law partner. Did this lead the senior Harlan to support the writ of habeas corpus? Nobody knows for certain, but Harlan did order that Debs and his associates be released on bail and referred their petition to the full Supreme Court for consideration.

The Supreme Court then ordered that formal appellate briefs be submitted by each side and that oral arguments be heard. Appellate briefs are relatively lengthy written arguments in which lawyers cite to the most significant precedents in support of their position. Oral arguments are, by contrast, actually presented orally; lawyers stand up before the justices and make their pitch in spoken words, often with the justices interrupting with questions and challenges. Both are customary when a case comes before the United States Supreme Court as well as before other appellate courts both in the federal system and in the individual states. Showing the type of respect for Trumbull that Gregory and Darrow had hoped for, the Supreme Court also took the unusual step of authorizing briefs and oral arguments by three lawyers on each side. The customary number of counsel at the time was two per side, but room had to be made for Trumbull.

The three defense attorneys went to work researching and drafting their appellate briefs. Their labors were prodigious, but in keeping with his more political role, the senior Trumbull's brief was the shortest—only eight pages. It in effect introduced the arguments that Gregory and Darrow would develop further. The initial point, Trumbull said, was that Debs and the American Railway Union had done nothing criminal and had not attempted to disrupt railroad service and the commerce that utilized the railroads. Their actions and statements were legal. What's more, Trumbull added in a point that ultimately would be greatly contested, the Chicago trial court had possessed no basis to enjoin the union. Since the injunction was improperly issued, the subsequent contempt citation for violating it was also invalid. The correct understanding of the powers of the Chicago court, Trumbull argued, should lead to a quick release for Debs and the other union officials.

The Gregory and Darrow appellate briefs, sixty-nine and ninety-seven pages in length respectively, were much more elaborate. Gregory pointed to the omnibus injunction that had already been criticized by some commentators and noted how ambiguous and open-ended some of its terms were. If general words of this sort were acceptable in an injunction, Gregory thought, the right to strike would be undermined. Allowing such an expansive injunction, Gregory suggested,

> will turn over the workingmen of this country, bound hand and foot, to the mercy of corporate rapacity and greed in a time when combination rules every market and every great enterprise and dominates all the activities of capital. The effect will be either to break the spirit of American wageworkers until they sink to a dull level but little above that of the dumb beasts; or else by continuing or restraining dynamic social forces until they gather an accumulated and resistless energy by such compression, precipitate an explosion which shall wreck the social order.

The Supreme Court, Gregory thought, should clearly affirm the right to strike. "It is idle to disguise or to dodge the question," he wrote. "This injunction was aimed at a strike; these men were imprisoned because they were leaders of a strike."

Hardly finished, Gregory went on to argue that Debs and his colleagues had been denied their rights as criminal defendants, in particular their right to a trial by jury. To allow the contempt proceeding to substitute for a criminal trial, he thought, would "weaken that respect for law which in a free state is always the chief security for social order." The defendants were entitled to a jury, and Gregory served up a long list of distinguished commentators who championed the jury trial as the cornerstone of Western freedoms. The case at hand, Gregory told the justices, was especially "dangerous because more covert and insidious." "Corporate and aggregated wealth," he asserted, was prepared to "sacrifice constitutional liberty upon the altar of the net earnings and exalt the interests of stockholders above the rights of man."

Gregory said in the last paragraph of his brief,

> No more tyrannous and arbitrary government can be devised than the administration of criminal law by a single judge by means of injunction and proceedings in contempt. To extend this power generally to criminal cases would be absolutely destructive to liberty and intolerable to a free people. It would be worse than ex post facto legislation. No man would be safe; no limits could be prescribed to the acts which might be forbidden nor the punishment to be inflicted.

Look to the law, Gregory told the Supreme Court in the kind of pontificating about law's identity that would run through the appellate process. "When the law is respected, when constitutional safeguards are maintained, though crime may sometimes escape punishment, at least innocence is secure."

Darrow matched Gregory citation for citation and rhetorical embellishment for rhetorical embellishment in his even lengthier brief. He referred specifically to the telegrams that had surfaced so frequently in the Chicago proceedings, saying they were perhaps the only thing that could be seen as a violation of the injunction. Note, Darrow hastily added, that the telegrams never urged violence or lawbreaking.

As for the single telegram that at least suggested violence, Darrow had his own read on it. Addressed to a man named Courthead in South Butte, Montana, the telegram said money should not be spent on potatoes or ice but rather on a gun. While testifying before the United States Strike Commission, American Railway Union representatives claimed that the telegram had been sent by a young clerk named Benedict to a friend and that even though signed "E. V. Debs," it was not an authorized union directive. Darrow did not rely on these claims in his appellate brief but argued the telegram was a harmless joke. "It would be doing violence to reason and common sense," Darrow wrote, "to say this telegram was meant to incite violence." Furthermore, the telegram was sent one day before the injunction appeared in the Chicago press and two days before the injunction was actually served.

Turning to Judge Woods's assertion that the Sherman Anti-Trust Act could be the basis for the injunction, Darrow cast the idea as preposterous. Congress had drafted and enacted the act with an eye toward addressing business combinations. Yes, strikes had also increased in number and magnitude as corporations and trusts had grown, but it was inconceivable, in Darrow's opinion, that Congress would have hoped to address strikes and unions through the Sherman Anti-Trust Act *and* not have mentioned it. The legislation, Darrow was sure, was "against capital."

Darrow concluded his brief by attempting to place the proceedings of the Chicago courts into a larger context, to share with the justices his sense of both history and the socioeconomic setting. The "industrial world," he said, "had been made over in the last fifty years." Theoretically, the laborer is now a "freeman, the equal of the employer, the equal of the lawyer or the judge." But, Darrow maintained, we know that the "great business princes" can purchase labor as a commodity at the lowest wages possible. Despite platitudes about the "harmony existing between capital and labor," we know "in actual life . . . these statements are not true." To deprive workingmen of the right to strike, Darrow insisted, would "strip and bind them and leave them helpless as the prey of the great and strong. It would be to despoil one army of every means of defense and aggression while in the field of battle, and in the presence of an enemy with boundless resources and all the equipments of warfare at their command."

––––––––

The chief representative of the opposing government side in the appeal to the Supreme Court was Attorney General Richard Olney. As will be discussed in the next chapter, Olney's involvement in the Pullman case led ultimately to slight modifications in his views. But he showed little sympathy for workers or unions during the strike, courtroom proceedings, and appeal to the Supreme Court.

Olney was a social Darwinist. Articulated by Yale professor William Graham Sumner and even more so by English thinker Herbert Spencer, social Darwinism extended Charles Darwin's theories of evolution to human social life. Social life had evolved naturally, the social Darwinists argued, and it would be counterproductive to disrupt this social evolution and aid the weak. Assets came to those who earned them, and social power rightfully came with those assets. "If we do not like survival of the fittest," Professor Sumner wrote, "we have only one possible alternative, and that is survival of the unfittest."

This made sense to Olney. Applying the theory to his own life, he was sure his diligent work on behalf of railroads and other corporate clients was what had enabled him to acquire not only his Commonwealth Avenue mansion but ultimately a twenty-six-room summer home on Martha's Vineyard as well. "Eminence at the bar," he thought, "is never the result of luck, nor of favoritism, nor of anything but sterling ability, sedulously devoted to the theory and practice of the law." He added in a graduation address,

> Man is by nature a fighting animal, and whether you look to the lives of individuals or the histories of nations, it is the fighters preeminently to whom is due the progress of the race. Collision, attrition, friction, are as necessary to bring out the best qualities of man as to develop the lustre and beauty of mahogany block or the gold or silver nugget.

It follows, he asserted with the logic of a social Darwinist, that "if there be failure, the fault will not be in your stars but in yourselves."

Perhaps predictably, Olney was a rigid man. Contemporaries described him as "icy," "formidable," and "difficult to approach," and Henry James, a biographer of the 1920s, offered an elaborate metaphor that makes one sit up and take notice. Olney, James said, was "a hard-thinking, accomplishing, ruthless being like one of those modern war-tanks which proceeds across the roughest ground, heedless of opposition, deaf alike to messages from friends and cries from the foe, able to crush every person and every obstacle that gets between it and its chosen objective." When Olney dictated to the indefatigable Miss Straw in his Boston law office, he sat behind a high rolltop desk, and she sat at a little table that he could not even see.

Relocated to Washington, D.C., to take charge of the Justice Department, Olney complained about the poor offices of the attorney general in a building on LaFayette Square. Fifty-nine years of age and beginning his third year on the cabinet, Olney invited nobody to call him by his first name. He wanted order, and he wanted respect. He wanted also to have his advice to President Cleveland to commit troops and his advice to Walker to obtain an injunction to be vindicated. He seemed, sometimes, to think he himself was on trial before the Supreme Court, and in his rigid and righteously contained way he was as passionately committed to prevailing in the appellate proceedings as were Gregory, Darrow, and Trumbull.

While during the Chicago proceedings Olney had privately pulled the strings, during the Washington, D.C., appeal he publicly grabbed the reins. Olney knew that Darrow had obtained the secret minutes of the General Managers' Association meetings that substantiated claims the railroads had attempted to reduce wages in conjunction with a larger antilabor policy. Olney knew as well, even before a juror became sick in February 1895, that the criminal prosecution was faltering. To minimize any impact on the proceedings before the Supreme Court, Olney therefore ordered Special Assistant United States Attorney Edwin Walker to proceed slowly with any efforts to remount the Chicago criminal conspiracy trial. Olney also urged United States attorneys in other parts of the country who still were pursuing criminal cases against strikers and boycotters to proceed slowly. Olney was concerned that actions against labor activists and leaders outside Chicago could jeopardize the government case involving events in Chicago that had now come before the Supreme Court.

Olney's chief assistants on the government side were a junior member of his Justice Department, Assistant Attorney General Edward B. Whitney, and the hardworking but often maligned Edwin Walker. Olney informed them and their staffs of a change in overall strategy. He wanted to emphasize jurisdictional matters, and in particular he wanted to move away from the emphasis Judge Woods in Chicago had placed on the Sherman Anti-Trust Act. Woods, Olney thought, had "decided rightly enough but upon the wrong ground." Refer to the Sherman Anti-Trust Act if you will, Olney told Whitney and Walker, but emphasize instead the general equity powers of the federal courts. If the Supreme Court would state unequivocally that the Chicago court had the power to issue an injunction, all questions about the meritoriousness of the strike, the right to strike, the use of armed forces, and the destruction of the American Railway Union would disappear.

In more specific terms, Whitney drew an assignment dear to the heart of an appellate proceduralist. Whitney was asked to and did in fact argue that the technical remedies sought from the Supreme Court were improper. In particular, his seven-page brief suggested the writ of habeas corpus was inappropriate because the Chicago contempt order was "interlocutory," that is, provisional or temporary rather than conclusive or final. Whitney had case citations to back up his argument, but as subsequent developments made clear, virtually no one thought this was the legal hook on which to hang the great Supreme Court appeal of the titanic struggle between labor and capital. Indeed, even Whitney's own appellate brief had a detectable sheepishness about arguing for dismissal on such refined questions of appellate procedure.

Edwin Walker had by this point fallen from Olney's favor, largely because of the delays and bad publicity for the government cause in Chicago. But Olney nevertheless gave Walker an assignment more interesting than Whitney's. Walker rose to the occasion with a well-crafted sixty-one-page brief, which largely argued that the Chicago court had indeed possessed the power to issue the injunction and then later cite Debs and his union colleagues for contempt when they violated the injunction.

Walker, of course, was so personally involved in the Chicago proceedings that he could not for a second have been expected to distance himself from them. He had a vested interest in arguing that the Chicago court had the power to do just what it had done. For one thing, he was sure that what was considered a "public nuisance" existed. Customarily, one sought to terminate such a "nuisance" by petitioning to a state rather than a federal court. But here the "nuisance" sprawled across state lines, and the federal courts were as a result the best place to seek relief. In addition, Walker wrote, the Chicago court must certainly have had the power to restrain interference with interstate commerce in and of itself. The railroads in this regard had become "the great public highways of the country," practically superseding the rivers as carriers of interstate commerce. Congress recognized this when in 1887 it enacted the Interstate Commerce Act, and this federal legislation, even though it did not explicitly address labor injunctions, surely enabled the Chicago court to act as it did. What's more, Walker asserted, the Supreme Court should be mindful of the United States mails. Even if the other bases for a court issuing an injunction were insufficient, a function of government such as the carriage of the mails had to be protectable. "Each and every letter, from the time it is deposited in the mail box provided by the government for its reception, until its delivery to the party or persons addressed," Walker said, echoing President Cleveland's earlier commitment to deliver even a postal card, "is wholly and exclusively within the control of the officers and agents of the government."

At the end of his brief Walker cut to what he no doubt took to be the quick. The petitioners were challenging the "authority of the government and the jurisdiction of the courts" to address an immense problem. The

Supreme Court had a "duty" to finally and authoritatively determine the jurisdiction of the circuit court, as will as the power of the government under the constitution and the law. "Similar conditions," Walker feared, "are likely to arise in the future." "Immediate protection of public rights, and the property rights of the government was imperative."

In still another fifty-nine-page appellate brief cosigned by Walker and Olney, the government attorneys reinforced their argument that the Chicago court had the jurisdictional power to issue an injunction and then find somebody in contempt for violating it. The government also strove once and for all to cut off misunderstandings of what the exercise of jurisdiction represented. The injunction was not a criminal prosecution. The actions of the workers, the strikers, and most certainly the union leaders were probably criminal conspiracies at common law, but, Walker and Olney contended, "It is not intended by us here to set forth the ancient and modern authorities upon the law of conspiracy." In addition, the injunction in and of itself did not speak to the right to strike. "It [the injunction] does not forbid a peaceful strike, nor does it forbid the exercise of all one's power to induce others, for any lawful purpose, to institute a peaceful strike. The only persuasion specifically enjoined is persuasion of employees remaining in their employment not to do their duty." The point, really, was to stop the massive interference with rail traffic and the mails, which had been "to the great detriment of the public." Walker and Olney were certain that a respected federal court with, among other things, recognizable equity jurisdiction had the power to enjoin this menace.

On March 25 and 26, 1895, the parties and lawyers appeared for oral arguments in the ornate Old Senate Chamber, where the Supreme Court sat during the 1890s. A century later, some have come to think that oral arguments are much less important than written appellate briefs, that the written word and its congruence with judicial preferences, rather than anything said in the courtroom, decides things on appeal. But in the nineteenth century, even in its final decade, oration and verbal eloquence were much more respected than today. Some of the largest figures in American culture and life were public speakers and lecturers. At minimum, oral arguments before the nineteenth-century Supreme Court constituted high and honorable drama. These arguments may also have changed minds and decided cases.

The galleries of the Old Senate Chamber were packed when the advocates for the two sides and the Supreme Court justices assembled for oral arguments in *In re Debs*. The *New York Times* reported, without venturing an explanation, that the audience included "an unusually large number of ladies." The *Chicago Tribune* was more expansive in its commentary. The galleries were overflowing. Standing room was at a premium. "Laboring people," the *Tribune* reported, "thronged every available nook and corner of the courtroom." These masses, the *Tribune* continued, were not happy. "It was the wish of the majority of those in attendance that all the grievances, real and fancied of the workingmen should have been aired by the advocates employed to defend President Debs." The masses in the galleries, it seems, "were not at all backward about expressing their opinions to this effect."

Contributing to the drama was the order in which the attorneys spoke and answered questions from the justices. Trumbull, Gregory, and Darrow did not immediately succeed one another at the lectern. Whitney, Walker, and Olney did not come forward one after the other. Instead, attorneys for the appellants and appellees alternated. Trumbull spoke first and was followed by Whitney. Gregory spoke next and was followed by Walker. Then, around 4:00 P.M. on the first day of the proceedings, the Court adjourned until the next day, at which time Olney offered the first oral argument, followed by Darrow. It was like a legal tennis match. One side stroked its best shot over the net, only to see the other side drive it back with equal power. The justices were not seated in chairs at courtside or stationed on the end lines. They were instead robed and sitting on high, and unlike tennis judges, the justices in fact participated with their comments and questions, their gestures and grimaces.

The oral arguments in and of themselves were even more passionate and personal than the appellate briefs. The opposing side was now more distinctly personified by the attorneys on the other side of the room. The legal battle was now more shaped and direct than it had been in the sprawling, multifaceted proceedings in Chicago. Furthermore, each side had now read the other side's appellate briefs and had a sense of how their adversaries were seeking to frame the legal issues. Arguments could now be anticipated and countered. When the *Chicago Tribune* reported that Darrow had responded to Olney with "some warmth," it was referring not to a sense of collegiality but rather to anger and irritation. All of the arguments, and the men who made them, were tense.

Trumbull rose first and declared that the primary object of the American Railway Union had been to bring about a peaceful adjustment between the Pullman Company and its employees. This praiseworthy goal would have been accomplished, he asserted, if it had not been for the refusal of Pullman officials to grant any concessions. Instead, we were left with the noxious injunction. The original statements that prompted the injunction were "reckless," and they had been sworn by an unknown person, a man who for all Trumbull knew had been picked up on the street for just this purpose. The injunction itself was also incorrect in saying that there was a boycott; furthermore, the injunction had been issued without notice, except in the newspapers. "If this was true, it was in defiance of Congress," Trumbull thundered, "as it was not to be supposed that everybody was to be compelled to read newspapers."

Whitney countered for the government, saying, in keeping with Olney's strategy of stressing jurisdiction, that he did not think it was necessary for the Supreme Court to resolve general questions of strikes and boycotts. This was "an untrodden field," he thought, and one on which the courts and text writers were divided. What Whitney did know was that great and irreparable injury had been done. The real question concerned the jurisdiction of a federal court sitting in equity, and he was sure the Chicago court had just what it had needed.

Gregory was next, and he argued for the defense that no one should lose sight of the way the very liberty of American citizens was at issue. His clients had ordered a strike, but they had not been enjoined from doing so. In fact, how could they be enjoined from doing what was their right? Regarding the jurisdiction that the government was determined to stress, Gregory asserted simply that there was none. No federal statute established any such jurisdiction, and to proceed as if the Sherman Anti-Trust Act had established such jurisdiction was to engage in "a kind of judicial strabism," that is, the type of distorted squinting necessary to combine two separated images into one. Showing an ever-greater awareness of Olney's precise strategic break from the Woods opinion, Gregory thought it telling that the government was now abandoning any reliance on the act.

Walker then spoke for the government and directly joined the jurisdictional issue. The federal court did not need a piece of specific federal legislation to sit in equity, he said. It had this power in and through its very existence. As a court of equity, the federal court could enjoin a nuisance, and it had properly issued an injunction in hopes of doing just that. With those thoughts from Walker, the time had reached 4:00 P.M., and the Supreme Court decided to adjourn until the next day.

On the next morning, March 26, the two sides changed their order, and the government went first, represented by Olney, with the defense represented by Darrow to follow. The press rightfully saw the speakers as a powerful two-part finale. Each appellate advocate had listened to the arguments of the previous day, and each had one last chance to get its side's most important arguments and counterarguments across. The very sight of the attorney general rising for oral argument was noteworthy. The solicitor general's position had been created in 1870, and in the 1890s as well as a century later, the solicitor general was chiefly responsible for arguing the government's position in appeals to the Supreme Court. The attorney general may occasionally appear, but on only two occasions during his entire tenure as attorney general did Olney make an oral argument.

This hardly meant Olney was ill-equipped or awkward, and commentators have described his efforts as "eloquent" and "brilliant." The "single question" before the Supreme Court, he announced, involved whether the court below had jurisdiction in the case. He was sure it did. He devoted little attention to discussing the strike itself, the government's relationship to the mails, or the provisions of the Sherman Anti-Trust Act, which he characterized as "an experimental piece of legislation." Think instead of interstate commerce, he said. Through historical evolution and recognition in federal legislation, steam railroads had become interstate commerce carriers. These carriers had been stopped, and it was as a result necessary for the government to do something.

"What was done," he said, awkwardly recalling the decisions of almost a year earlier, "was done on a conspicuous theater and dealt with events striking in themselves and in the scale on which they were conducted." The events, he said with an inevitable shrug, "strongly appealed to the imagination as well as the passions of men." The government action was denounced from the outset as novel and unprecedented, "so that it even became expedient to publicly proclaim the trite and familiar principle that for the executions of national functions every foot of every State is national soil and national property." Since then the government bill in equity, the injunction, and the proceeding for contempt had also "been loudly condemned as anomalous, extraordinary, and revolutionary." "To such charges," Olney said in conclusion, "there could be no more decisive answer than is furnished by this debate and by the contentions of the respective parties."

As Darrow waited his turn to reply, he may have soberly noticed that during the full duration of Olney's argument not a single member of the Supreme Court had interrupted or questioned him. All of the justices, the *Chicago Tribune* reported, had given Olney "the closest attention." As the final speaker in the oral arguments, Darrow faced a task at least difficult, and perhaps impossible.

Darrow opened by saying he agreed with the attorney general that the case was one of vast importance. Not only was it of importance to the corporation, it was of importance to millions of working people. The attorney general, Darrow asserted, had overlooked the interests of the latter, as he had overlooked the danger to civil liberty embraced by the case. With a bit of sour grapes, Darrow criticized the government for abandoning its reliance on the Sherman Anti-Trust Act, and he added that interstate commerce legislation was also irrelevant for jurisdiction purposes because it was simply railroad regulation.

Darrow then made a lengthy personal appeal on behalf of his clients. They were not criminals, and their acts were not criminal. He could say on behalf of them that, although they might have been misguided and unwise, they had acted from the highest and purest motives:

> When a body of 100,000 men lay down their implements of labor, not because their own rights have been invaded, but because the bread has been taken from the mouths of their fellows, we have no right to say that they are criminals. It is difficult for us to place ourselves in the position of others, but this Court should endeavor to do so and should realize that the petitioners in this case are representatives of the great laboring element of this country upon which this country must so largely depend for its safety, prosperity and progress.

When Darrow concluded, the Supreme Court adjourned, but unbelievably the evening found the attorneys together again. Attorney General Olney hosted a dinner party for Trumbull, Gregory, Darrow, and the ladies who had come with them to Washington, D.C. Whitney and Walker attended, as did Chief Justice Fuller. Olney later noted that Debs's attorneys were quite surprised as well as pleased at the attention, as they had apparently gotten the impression that as representatives of Debs, they would not be considered within the pale of respectable Washington society. The legalists had earnestly and passionately made their best arguments, and now as fellow members of the bar, they could tip their glasses to one another and reflect on their lawyerly prowess.

––––––––

On Monday, May 27—almost exactly two months after the oral arguments—the Supreme Court announced and formally read its opinion. Although the government lawyers and the Chicago federal courts had been sharply criticized by some members of the press and in certain circles of the bar, a ruling against Debs and his colleagues was fully expected. Trumbull, Gregory, and Darrow had been more than competent in their appellate briefs and oral arguments, but—the stirring nature of their prolabor rhetoric notwithstanding—they had not rocked the core legal arguments of the government regarding equity jurisdiction. The Supreme Court had given no signs during the oral arguments that Debs and the American Railway Union might for a second be expected to prevail.

Chosen to write the opinion was Justice David J. Brewer. The son of a Congregationalist missionary from Massachusetts, Brewer had been born in Smyra, Asia Minor, where his father was attempting to convert Jews and Greeks to the distinctive propositions of New England-style Protestantism. Brewer's mother was Emilia Field—the sister of Henry M. Field, a noted clergyman; of Cyrus W. Field, the man who laid the Atlantic cable; of David Dudley Field, author of the "Field Code" and legal codifier; and of Stephen J. Field, prominent California jurist. Against the backdrop of what must sometimes have seemed an avuncular sibling rivalry run amuck, young David J. Brewer graduated from Yale College, studied law with his uncle David Dudley Field, and then decided to make his own name and fortune in Kansas. After distinguishing himself as a lawyer, judge, and member of the Kansas Supreme Court, Brewer was nominated in 1889 to the United States Supreme Court, where, lest he think he now stood on his own accomplishments, his uncle Stephen J. Field was already a member. A confident Republican and supporter of American business interests, Brewer had lived in Washington, D.C., and served on the Court for just over five years when he penned the *In re Debs* opinion.

Brewer was sanguine about the opinion-writing task. Nobody forced him to speak to the matter. The nation's industrial unrest and the ongoing struggle between capital and labor had troubled him deeply. The Pullman strike and boycott in particular had made his temperature rise.

In 1894, in keeping with duties of Supreme Court justices of the era, he had temporarily joined the circuit court and penned the *Ames v. Pacific Railway Company* opinion. Alluding to the Pullman strike and boycott, Brewer deemed them "fearful struggles." Perhaps the law could make sense of what had transpired and rule in ways that would preclude such developments in the future.

Brewer began his opinion in *In re Debs* by indicating what he took to be the two important questions of the case. The first involved the federal government's ability to prevent obstructions of interstate commerce and of transportation of the mails. The second concerned the power of a federal court acting through its equity jurisdiction to issue an injunction in support of efforts to protect interstate commerce and the delivery of the mails. The choice of questions to ask is often indicative of the answers one plans to provide. If somehow Trumbull, Gregory, and Darrow still harbored hopes that they had prevailed against Olney and his charges, Brewer's opening questions should have quashed those hopes once and for all. The Supreme Court was indeed heading toward a justification of the steps taken by the federal government to end the strike and boycott.

As for his first question, Brewer was convinced that the Constitution had unambiguously given the federal government powers relating to interstate commerce and the mails. Echoing arguments in the appellate brief written by Edwin Walker, Brewer noted that Congress had used these powers to legislate, and, he went on to add, that was hardly the end of things. "The entire strength of the nation may be used to enforce in any part of the land the full and free exercise of all national powers and the security of all rights entrusted by the Constitution to its care," he said. "The strong arm of the national government," he continued, "may be put forth to brush away all obstructions to the freedom of interstate commerce or the transportation of the mails." The "strong arm," in Brewer's terms, included the army and the state militia—just the forces that had been mustered against the strikers.

Turning to the second of his original questions, Brewer provided the unequivocal statement regarding the powers of the Chicago court that Olney had wanted:

Grant that any public nuisance may be forcibly abated either at the instance of the authorities, or by any individual suffering private damage therefrom, the existence of this right of forcible abatement is not inconsistent with nor does it destroy the right of appeal in an orderly way to the courts for a judicial determination, and an exercise of their powers by writ of injunction and otherwise accomplish the same result.

Stated more simply: The federal government could seek an injunction, and the court had the power to grant it. Brewer went on,

Indeed, it is more to the praise than the blame of the government, that, instead of determining for itself questions of right and wrong on the part of these petitioners and their associates and enforcing that determination by the club of the policeman and the bayonet of the soldier, it submitted all those questions to the peaceful determination of judicial tribunals.

What's more, resonating with this determination, the great body of workers and strikers respected the judgment of the courts and ceased their disruptive conduct.

Lest this latter point be overlooked, Brewer quoted, without naming, none other than Debs himself. The courts, Debs had said, had been much more important than the military, and judicial orders were what had broken the strike. "It was not the soldiers that ended the strike. It was not the old brotherhoods that had ended the strike. It was simply the United States courts that ended the strike." Brewer liked this language. He saw it as welcome acknowledgment. In the context of industrial America, the courts were and should be powerful ordering institutions even for dissenters, malcontents, and troublemakers.

At the very end of the decision, formal holdings having already been offered, Brewer detoured into even more overt lecturing about law generally and abstractly understood. Referring back to the appellate arguments and especially to the very final words from Darrow on behalf of the defense, Brewer cited "the most earnest and eloquent appeal in eulogy of the heroic spirit of those who threw up their employment, and gave up their means of earning a livelihood, not in defense of their own rights, but in sympathy for and to assist others whom they believed to be wronged." Heroism and self-sacrifice were to be admired, Brewer said, but

it is a lesson which cannot be learned too soon or too thoroughly under this government of and by the people that the means of redress of all wrongs are through the courts and at the ballot-box, and that no wrong, real or fancied, carries with it legal warrant to invite as a means of redress the cooperation of a mob, with its accompanying acts of violence.

The workers, strikers, and union leaders had been wrong; more generally, in industrial America labor and capital should settle their disputes in the courts and in the legislatures with reference to the overarching rule of law.

Having finished their work, the justices of the Supreme Court retired to their chambers, but their decision in *In re Debs* prompted many to come forward with public comment. The press both solicited the opinions of those who had participated in the appellate process and also offered its editorial observations. The cavalcade of comments ranged from the rawest and most overtly political statements to the most elevated and abstracted comments on law.

Some participants on both sides saw the decision in political terms. For Debs himself, the decision made particular sense when coupled with another recent Supreme Court decision declaring unconstitutional a federal income tax. "Both decisions," Debs said, "are absolutely in the interest of the corporations, syndicates, and trusts, which dominate every department of the Federal Government, including the Supreme Court." "Railroad corporations may now reduce wages and enforce any kind of conditions upon their employees without fear of resistance. If employees see fit to quit, they can be put in jail for exercising this prerogative." Furthermore, Debs complained, "Every Federal Judge is now made a Czar. The decision of the Supreme Court had crowned them and given them autocratic sway."

On the other end of the political spectrum, just the ramifications that so troubled Debs registered as welcome. George R. Peck, the chairman of the General Managers' Association legal committee, immediately wired a robustly congratulatory message to Olney. "The Supreme Court seems to agree with you," Peck quipped, "that the soil of Illinois is the soil of the United States." District Attorney Milchrist, who had in Chicago played a major role in securing the contempt citation and also helped in the criminal prosecution, thought the decision defined "the strength of the United States Circuit Court in cases where strikers quit work, assemble in riotous mobs and forcibly prevent others from working." "The Supreme Court in upholding the decision of Judge Woods," Milchrist was relieved to see, "has placed a great barrier to such scenes as saw in the great railroad strike a year ago."

More rabid than the railroad representatives and the prosecutors was the *Chicago Tribune*. Throughout the strike and boycott and also during the

Chicago courtroom proceedings, the *Tribune* had never wavered in its condemnation of Debs, the American Railway Union, and labor in general. Now, the *Tribune* could gleefully announce that

> whatever else may be interfered with there will be no more attempts except on the part of train robbers to stop the transportation of the mails or to tie up inter-State commerce. There will be no more insurrections like that of last July. No so-called 'labor leaders' will endeavor to block the wheels of commerce in order to bring pressure to bear on some private corporation.

Building political steam, the *Tribune* said that the decision was "a notice to all Anarchists and other disturbers of the peace that the hands of the General Government are not fettered." And the newspaper even took a potshot at its least-admired governor by adding as well that "The Supreme Court has decided that Altgeld was a presumptuous intermeddler."

Beyond the political complaining and boasting, some chose to comment on the more recognizably legal aspects of the decision, but, here too, room existed for personalized reactions. Trumbull, for example, greeted the decision with nothing less than disgust, and he complained than the legal doctrine that the Supreme Court had chosen and reaffirmed gave too much power to federal judges. Judge Woods, on the other hand, was pleased that his own understanding of the injunction and contempt citation had been upheld, although he seemed not to appreciate that the legal grounds had shifted from the ones he had emphasized. *In re Debs,* Woods admitted honestly, was "highly gratifying." He now knew he "was right in issuing the injunction last summer against the officers of the American Railway Union, and being right in the law the right to punish the men for contempt followed as a natural sequence."

The greatest horn-tooting about the legal frame chosen by the Supreme Court came from the attorney general. Olney had never really thought much of the opposing counsel and claimed to be surprised "by their rather obvious avoidance of the crucial legal problem involved and their resort to heated declamations about individual liberty, the right to trial by jury, etc., etc." The best opposing arguments, Olney thought, had been made by Gregory, who at least had been "professionally retained and paid." Fortunately, Olney immodestly and with substantial accuracy told the loyal Miss Straw, the Supreme Court "took my argument and turned it into an opinion."

The *New York Times* had predicted confidently how the case would be decided, and it was almost as pleased as Olney with the frame the Supreme Court had chosen. "Henceforth, whenever the General Government, acting under a Constitutional law, applies for and receives an order of a United States court to enjoin resistance to the law," the *Times* announced, "the whole power of the Nation is made available to enforce that order." The unanimous decision was particularly significant, the *Times* thought, "considering the membership of the Court as to parties and as to sectional distribution."

What did the decision say about law understood most philosophically and abstractly? The comments on this score in the appellate briefs, in the oral arguments, and in the final opinion itself had undeniably been as much ideological as jurisprudential. Darrow and Walker continued to strike the same tone when all had been said and done. Darrow believed the decision coupled law with arbitrary power, a step he considered extremely dangerous. *In re Debs*, he thought, "left the law so biased that, in cases involving strikes, at least, a man could be sent to prison for crime without trial by jury." The much maligned Walker, meanwhile, at least had a moment on what he took to be the highest road. "All that was contended for by the government," he said, "was the supremacy of the law."

CHAPTER 5

Ramifications and Conclusions

The *In re Debs* opinion written by Justice David Brewer for the United States Supreme Court in 1895 was not crucial in ending the Pullman strike and boycott. In Chicago, the presence of federal troops, the labor injunction, and the arrest of American Railway Union leaders for the alleged violation of the injunction ended the rioting and tumult by July 12, 1894. One by one the other twenty-six states that had experienced disruption and worse calmed. By the middle of July, all observers knew that the strike and boycott had failed. On July 17, the *Daily Inter Ocean* reported that federal troops had been ordered to leave Chicago and also that workers had begun to return to their jobs at the Pullman car works. Capital with the assistance of government or, if one prefers the reverse, government with the assistance of capital had defeated labor.

Yet while little ambiguity existed regarding the results of the great strike and boycott, the entire Pullman case—stretching from the initial walkout of the workers on May 11, 1894, to the rendering of the Supreme Court decision on May 27, 1895—had additional significance and ramifications. The case directly affected the lives and careers of the major participants, and in that sense carried forward for decades. Furthermore, the case had lasting importance for labor and capital and for law and legal institutions. All of these matters merit consideration in this concluding chapter, as does the still larger question of what the case tells us about the very nature of law in the context of industrializing America.

Thinking of the major participants in the Pullman case, one might place them into three categories: (1) representatives of capital, (2) representatives of labor, and (3) legal advocates and officers. Bright lines do not separate the categories. In particular, legal officers, as previous chapters have suggested, often seemed committed to and even affiliated with capital. However, these officers at least definitionally represented the people of the United States or of individual states rather than one of the sides in the immense struggle.

The most important representatives of capital in the Pullman controversy were the General Managers' Association and George Pullman. While individual railroads did what they could to keep their lines operating, the managers' group took the lead position for capital. The association's executive decision makers, attorneys, and detectives played aggressive and critical roles in breaking the strike and, even more so, in the undermining of the boycott. The mainstream media of the period did not devote as much attention to the work of the managers' group as it did to the efforts of other institutional and individual participants in the controversy. But the commission appointed by President Cleveland to investigate the strike did appreciate both the effectiveness and the questionable conduct of the General Managers' Association.

Headed by Carroll D. Wright, the United States commissioner of labor, and including John D. Kernan of New York and Nicholas E. Worthington of Chicago, the commission held hearings in Washington, D.C., and Chicago in the late summer of 1894. In particular, the commissioners summoned and aggressively questioned Everett St. John, the chairman of the managers' group, and John M. Egan, the leader of the its antistrike activities. Later, St. John and Egan were quoted and the General Managers' Association was discussed in the lengthy report delivered to the president in November 1894.

For starters, the commission wondered if the General Managers' Association had "any legal authority, statutory or otherwise" to set rates and wages for participating railroads or to battle strikes as it had. "It is a usurpation of power not granted," the commission stated bluntly. Extrapolating further, the commission thought the managers' group's efforts were "an illustration of the persistent and shrewdly designed plans of corporations to overreach their limitations and usurp indirectly powers and rights not contemplated in their charters and not obtainable from the people or their legislators." A continuation of this sort of activity, the commission felt, was "an aggregation of power and capital dangerous to the people and their liberties." Keep it up, the commission warned the association, the railroads, and capital in general, and you will soon find yourself with government ownership of the railroads.

As for the conduct of the managers' group during the strike and boycott itself, the commission was equally critical. It condemned the association for refusing in advance to receive any communications from the American Railway Union and for returning communications unanswered. "The refusal of the General Managers' Association to deal with such a combination of labor as the American Railway Union," the commission said, "seems arrogant and absurd." The commission also deplored the refusal to even consider arbitration, a stance that closed the door to attempts at conciliation and settlement. "The commission is impressed with the belief, by the evidence and by the attendant circumstances as disclosed," the commissioners stated, "that a different policy would have prevented the loss of life and great loss of property and wages occasioned by the strike."

While the managers' association had been aggressive in attempting to counter the national boycott and attempting to justify their actions, George Pullman's chief goal during the strike and boycott seemed frequently to be avoiding visibility. He left Chicago as soon as possible after the social disorder began. He dodged having to testify in the criminal conspiracy prosecution. He declared that things were not in his hands but in those of the federal government and courts.

None of these steps succeeded fully in shielding Pullman from the public spotlight, and the hearings conducted by the strike commission undoubtedly were especially painful for him. Along with Thomas Wickes, the same company vice president who had held the line against the strikers in the early days of the strike, Pullman appeared before the commission on August 27, 1894. The commissioners questioned him combatively, asking about annual profits, the company's capitalization, and the relation of profit to capitalization. The commissioners also wanted to know how much time Pullman actually spent in his town. For his own part, Pullman reiterated his position that wages and rents were separate matters. He repeated the earlier assertion that his company simply could not afford to pay the workers more than it did. The testimony suggests Pullman had not been able to move beyond his own positions in the strike to a broader or longer view. Pullman remained convinced that he had been right in how he had handled things.

The commission did not see it that way. The commissioners observed in their final report that since Pullman had obtained his corporate charter in 1867, the company had put aside $25 million in surplus earnings. This lordly surplus, one might have thought, would have led to concessions regarding wages and rents. Instead, when the economy turned sour in the early 1890s, the company pushed a disproportionate amount of its losses onto the workers. The company did not reduce the salaries of executives or even superintendents, but such cuts, even though they would have been felt less severely, would have demonstrated concern with and sympathy for the workers. The very act of staying open with severe wage reductions in the midst of an economic downturn, the commissioners said, was economically advantageous. Despite the absence of profit, the company maintained its fleet of railroad cars, prevented deterioration of its industrial plant, scared off would-be competitors, and stationed itself for resumed production once the demand for Pullman cars reappeared.

And through all of this, the commissioners noted, rents remained high, higher in fact than the rents for comparable housing in adjacent towns. The company's claim that its workers did not have to live in Pullman was false, at least to the extent that the company gave preferential treatment to renters when company fortunes faltered. The company had a "legal right" to insist on high rents and refuse to lower them, but "as between man and man the demand for some rent reduction was fair and reasonable under all the circumstances." Some slight concession in this area, the commission suggested, might even have averted the strike.

Beyond reduced wages and high rents—the economic nuts and bolts of Pullman's policy in the months preceding the strike—Pullman failed also to respect the workers' needs for self-expression and independence. His refusal to recognize unions was "behind the age," and the disdain for workers' complaints, demands, and requests for arbitration was insulting. In commenting on the low subscription rates for the town library, the commissioners said, "It is possible that the air of business strictly maintained there, as elsewhere, as well as the exclusion from any part of its management prevent more universal and grateful acceptance of its advantages by employees. Men, as a rule, even when employees, prefer independence to patriotism in such matters." The commission found "on the one side a very wealthy and unyielding corporation, and upon the other a multitude of employees of comparatively excellent character and skill, but without local attachments or any interested responsibility in the town, its businesses, its tenements, or surroundings."

The commission did conclude that the workers' demand at the time of the strike for a return to 1893 wages was unreasonable, but this hardly counteracted the image of a rich manufacturer who had made an immense fortune in his time and then used the excuse of an economic downturn to continue his exploitative, paternalistic treatment of labor. This appraisal must have made Pullman sick, and, indeed, his health did literally begin to fail during the strike, boycott, and commission hearings. There were ups and downs, signs of hope and reasons for concern for three years. But then, on October 19, 1897, Pullman suffered a horrifying heart attack. Servants summoned the family physician, but nothing could be done. Pullman's wife, Hattie, received the news of her husband's death while on still another of her trips to New Jersey, and she raced back to Chicago in the trains and specialty cars so central to the Pullman fortune.

Pullman's will treated Hattie and his daughters well. Hattie received the mansion on Prairie Avenue in Chicago along with $50,000 in immediate cash and the continuing income on a fund of $1.25 million. Pullman's daughters, Florence and Harriet, divided the other major properties, and each also received the income on a $1 million fund and residual bequests of $3 million. Pullman's twin sons, by contrast, received one last admonition from their father. Dissatisfied with the twins' drinking and failure to settle into careers, Pullman left each a piddling $3,000 per year. By the time the will went to probate in 1900, the estate had grown in value to $17.5 million, and the twins tried unsuccessfully to enlarge their shares of the sizable assets.

Pullman's will both extended his paternalism toward his workers and showed the way they haunted him even at death. The paternalism is evident in the bequests Pullman made to a dozen charitable organizations in Chicago and, especially, in the whopping $1.25 million he left to his town of Pullman. He directed that the money be spent on a manual training school for the children of his workers. In later years corporate executives have been known to endow college scholarships instead, but in Pullman's time manual training funds could be understood as beneficent.

Much stranger than the bequests were Pullman's directions for his burial. For a few years prior to his death, he had been obsessed with the fear that the men he had defeated in the strike and boycott would snatch and desecrate his corpse. Hence, he ordered that morticians place his body in a special casket wrapped in tar paper and coated with asphalt. The casket was lowered into a grave thirteen feet long, nine feet wide, and eight feet deep. The floor of the grave was concrete, and once the casket came to rest on it, a crew of men filled the spaces around and on top of the casket with still more concrete.

While Pullman's corpse was presumably safe for all time, his reputation was not. He had defeated his workers, Debs, the American Railway

Union, and labor in general, but Pullman did not want to be known as a man who could crush labor. Recalling the development and promotion of his model town, we know he was driven by more than a desire to make money. Pullman had a social vision. His company and the condition and behavior of his workers were to be standards both for the industrial sector and for the society as a whole. Professor Ely had perceived flaws in the vision as early as the mid-1880s, and the strike and boycott, even though defeated, sharply brought the flaws into higher relief. The resulting irony was that the man who fancied himself progressive emerged as old-fashioned and even reactionary. His vision of industrial and social harmony came to register as one of industrial and social control. His efforts to lift up his workers seemed to many an effort to hold them down.

Jane Addams, the Hull House reformer whose comments on the initial strike had been so perceptive, also had an insightful interpretation of Pullman himself. Pullman, she suggested in a talk delivered to the Chicago Women's Club, the Twentieth-Century Club of Boston, and other audiences, was "a modern Lear." Like the Shakespearean character who was concerned with the well-being of his daughter Cordelia, Pullman was concerned with the well-being of his workers. Both the Shakespearean Lear and the modern one, meanwhile, were unwilling to give their "children" any voice in the shaping of their lives. Both wanted total loyalty, but both failed to respect the preferences and aspirations of their self-styled charges. Pullman, in particular, failed to recognize the situation that the concentration of capital had created for labor in industrial America. Instead of closing the gaps between capital and labor, he had demanded that labor accept his terms and his judgment. When his "children" failed to see things his way, Addams said, "the shock of disaster upon egotism" produced palpable "self-pity."

While George Pullman, the winner, saw his vision destroyed as a result of the Pullman case, Eugene Debs, the loser, found a new vision. As early as July 11, 1894—a mere week after federal troops entered Chicago—Debs acknowledged privately that the strike and boycott were failing. He told Pullman the workers would return on the latter's terms. He asked the General Managers' Association to arbitrate. He called on Mayor Hopkins of Chicago for help. Nothing worked. Debs announced that "every avenue has been closed. . . . So far as we are concerned, we feel like the boy who

was kicked by the jackass. We just consider the source from which it came."
The American Railway Union disbanded, and many of Debs's loyal union-
ists found themselves blacklisted.

Debs's immediate destination was the jail in Woodstock, to which he
had been sent earlier when Judge Woods found him in contempt for violating the injunction. He and the other union leaders who had lost their
appeal to the United States Supreme Court were supposed to report as a
group on June 11, 1895, but Debs arrived a day later than the others, claim-
ing that he had become ill from "eating cucumbers." Somewhat miracu-
lously, he seemed free of venom. After settling in at Woodstock, he actually
wrote to Attorney General Olney, requesting a copy of the latter's appellate brief for inclusion in a souvenir volume he was preparing. In later years
as well, Debs told acquaintances that despite all that happened, he considered Olney an honorable man.

More significantly, Debs moved from his disappointing and disastrous
experiences in the direction of socialist politics. Given the presence of
socialist ideas in late-nineteenth-century American progressive circles, it is
unlikely that his imprisonment was the very first occasion for Debs to wrestle
with socialist thought. Indeed, right after Justice Brewer announced the
United States Supreme Court decision in *In re Debs,* Debs hinted of socialism. "I shall abide by the decision with perfect composure," he said, "confidently believing that it will hasten the day of public ownership, not only of
the railroads, but of all other public utilities. I view it as the death knell of
the wage system." Always able to put a positive spin on things, Debs hoped
the decision "in the long run . . . will prove a blessing to the country."

While imprisoned, Debs gave more and more thought to the socialist
critique of industrial capitalism. He reported being impressed by the writings of Karl Kautsky, a popularizer of Karl Marx's thought. Kautsky, Debs
said, was "so clear and conclusive that I readily grasped, not merely his
argument, but also caught the spirit of his Socialist utterance." Victor
Berger, the leader of Milwaukee's burgeoning socialist movement, one
which came eventually to dominate the city's politics for half a century,
visited Debs in Woodstock. Berger gave Debs a copy of *Das Kapital* and, in
Debs's words, "delivered the first impassioned messages of Socialism I had
ever heard—the very first to set the 'wires humming in my system.'" Having earlier moved from conventional civic attitudes and the brotherhoods
to a more critical stance and industrial unionism, Debs was ready to take
still another step even further to the left.

Not long after completing his prison term, Debs endorsed William Jennings Bryan for president. Bryan had won the 1896 nomination of both the Democratic Party and the Populist Party, and Debs presumably had some special fondness for planks in the Democratic Party's platform deploring labor injunctions and life tenure for federal judges. However, Debs was not particularly active in the campaign and seems never to have become a genuinely devoted Bryanite.

On January 1, 1897, Debs formally announced his adoption of the socialist position that had been percolating in his mind since the Supreme Court decision. Writing in an open letter in the *Railway Times,* Debs stated that he had never taken Bryan's emphasis on the free coinage of silver to be a panacea for inequality in the industrial sector. The recently completed presidential election in which William McKinley defeated Bryan, Debs said, showed that the ballot in and of itself was unlikely to produce emancipation from wage slavery. He cast the economic system as "cannibalistic, with men set one against another," and he left no doubt were he had come to stand: "The issue is, Socialism vs. Capitalism. I am for Socialism because I am for humanity. We have been cursed with the reign of gold long enough. Money constitutes no proper basis of civilization. The time has come to regenerate society—we are on the verge of a universal change."

In subsequent years, Debs's acceptance of socialism following the Pullman case and his Woodstock imprisonment became one of the great fables of American socialism, and Debs himself emerged as the leader of the movement. Thousands of Americans who became socialists in quieter and less public ways vicariously identified with Debs. Debs's political conversion story became an archetype.

Later in 1897 Debs abandoned all hope of revitalizing the American Railway Union and formally dissolved the organization. He and several other leaders of the defunct union then helped found Social Democracy of America, and the latter evolved into the Socialist Party of America The party chose Debs to be its presidential candidate on five occasions. He of course never came close to occupying the White House, although he did in 1912 garner 6 percent of the national vote. His total of 919,799 votes in 1920 was also remarkable if one bears in mind that he ran for president while imprisoned in the Atlanta Federal Penitentiary, where he had been sentenced for opposing United States participation in World War I.

More important than Debs's vote totals was the great respect many Americans came to have for him. Americans perceived him as a man of principle and integrity. Tributes at the time of his death in 1926 came from all points on the political spectrum. Even bestowed with the hard-earned respect of many, though, Debs himself did not abandon the harder-edged politics he adopted after the Pullman strike and courtroom proceedings. Not long before his death, he commented on the Massachusetts Supreme Court's refusal to grant a new trial to Sacco and Vanzetti. "The decision of this capitalist judicial tribunal is not surprising," he said. "It accords perfectly with the tragical farce and farcical tragedy of the entire trial of these two absolutely innocent and shamefully persecuted working men."

―――――――

The lawyers who worked on the Pullman case—Richard Olney, Edwin Walker, Thomas M. Milchrist, Edward B. Whitney, William W. Erwin, Stephen Gregory, Clarence Darrow, and Lyman Trumbull, among others—constituted a tremendous assembly of late-nineteenth-century legal talent. Had they somehow been able to see eye-to-eye on things, they could have made up the era's single most accomplished and impressive law firm. They could have wowed clients and the courts and made themselves a bundle. For several of these lawyers, Edwin Walker and Lyman Trumbull for example, involvement in the Pullman case came toward the end of long, successful careers and in some sense capped those careers. Others went on to other pursuits, deriving lessons from the Pullman case that would serve and shape them in the future.

Richard Olney, of course, had served as United States attorney general during the strike and boycott and led government efforts during the subsequent legal proceedings. As attorney general, he was charged with representing the people, but, as suggested in earlier chapters, his long affiliation with the railroads prevented neutral decision making. Indeed, Olney even continued to receive retainers from several railroads while serving as attorney general, an arrangement that had raised eyebrows in the press and in Congress.

One of Olney's first steps after the American Railway Union had been defeated was in fact to reduce his connections to the railroads. During the summer of 1894, after the strike had ended but before legal proceedings in the case had concluded, Olney stopped drawing his quarterly salary of twenty-five thousand dollars from the Chicago, Burlington and Quincy Railroad Company. He continued, however, to advise the railroad company and serve without compensation on its board of directors. Olney also during the summer of 1894 more or less severed his ties with the Atchison, Topeka & Santa Fe Railroad Company, turning his work over to another attorney whom he himself had chosen. These moves and others were amicable, and Olney no doubt assumed he had not burned his bridges with the railroads. He could ultimately return to his high-paid legal practice on behalf of the railroads after completing his service as attorney general.

Beyond attempting to eliminate questions about whether he worked for the government or the railroads, Olney also looked into whether other government representatives had untoward ties to the railroads. Olney had been stung in this regard by charges in the strike commission report that his own Justice Department had used loyal railroad employees as United States marshals during the strike. The railroads, the strike commission asserted, had not only selected these men but also fed, housed, armed, supervised, and paid them. The men, the commission added, "acted in the double capacity of railroad employees and United States officers." This placed officers of the government "under contract of a combination of railroads. It is a bad precedent, that might lead to serious consequences."

This could not really have happened, Olney thought. He contemplated an attack on the commission for so badly misrepresenting the government's relationship to the railroads, an attack that given Olney's style would most certainly have been blistering. But just before he opened fire, Olney received reports from Milchrist and Walker and also from George B. Harris, vice president of the Chicago, Burlington and Quincy, confirming the charges. Roughly thirty-six hundred railroad employees had served as marshals. Milchrist argued that the "turbulence, violence and lawlessness" of the strike had justified the action, but Olney believed in "these ever recurring and ever intensifying collisions between labor and capital" the government "should not only be impartial in fact but impartial in appearance also." We want to avoid the charge, he said, that the government "is nothing but the paid agent and instrument of capital." Truly upset by what he had uncovered, Olney ordered that the railroads be repaid for the money they had paid to employees turned marshals.

Most surprisingly, Olney as a result of the Pullman case also began grudgingly to rethink his positions on the relations of railroad capital and labor. Fiercely dogmatic and confident to a fault, he never in the past had been a man to change his tune. One would not have expected flexibility from him. But at the same time, Olney had never really been a railroad *labor* lawyer. As noted earlier, his real specialty was railroad mergers and acquisitions. The Pullman strike and proceedings, therefore, were a ragged introduction to the subject of labor relations. Indeed, they may have been Olney's introduction to labor in general. According to Olney's modern biographer, the only working-class people Olney even talked to before the Pullman strike were his servants. "A terrible night for the poor people," the maudlin Olney would say to his family on cold winter evenings in Boston. Only through his involvement in the Pullman strike did Olney come to reflect on the condition of labor.

In the summer of 1894 Olney engaged in correspondence with United States Supreme Court Justice John Marshall Harlan, the same justice who would six months later refer the habeas corpus petition to the full Supreme Court for consideration. Olney said in the correspondence that injunctions were sometimes going to be necessary in labor struggles, but perhaps recalling the calm that had reigned in Pullman itself throughout the strike and boycott, Olney rejected the idea that strikes themselves were inherently lawless and prone to violence. Furthermore, Olney told Harlan, railroad workers might have a right to strike, depending on the circumstances and the amount of notice given to their employers.

Subsequently, Olney reached even firmer conclusions about the right to strike. In September of 1894, he opposed an order from the Philadelphia & Reading Railroad that all employees resign union membership or be fired. He filed an amicus brief in November of the same year, arguing that a requirement that men quit a union was unfair because it would deprive them of union benefits. Strikes in and of themselves, Olney said clearly, were not illegal; only violent or otherwise injurious strikes could be stopped. To outlaw all strikes, he concluded, would be to invite chronic discontent among workers who saw that capital was much freer to organize and act together than labor was. A ban on strikes would convince workers that the law itself had "taken sides against them."

Just how might railroad capital and labor get along? Olney endorsed the possibility of courts serving as arbiters between railroads and their workers. If one bears in mind how sympathetic most courts, especially in the federal system, were to capital, this was not as balanced a position as it may first appear. But still, Olney had moved beyond a blind commitment to capital and its control of workers, with the courts as simply instruments of control.

The Pullman strike commission, incidentally, had also endorsed some variety of arbitration, and two of the commissioners submitted a draft of proposed arbitration legislation to the labor committee of the House of

Representatives. Olney did not support this draft, in large part because it proposed a permanent arbitration board, but he did submit his own draft to Congress. Some of the traditional brotherhoods supported the bill, and it passed in the House. The Senate, where the sway of capital was greatest, was less receptive.

It would have been interesting, given Olney's prestige and his position as attorney general, if he had able to pursue his thinking and legislative proposals further. No one viewed him as a labor advocate, and as a result his views on arbitration might have received careful attention. But alas, other demands for his time intervened. For starters, the appeal of the Pullman case dominated his thinking during the first half of 1895, and Olney could not refrain from seeing the appeal as an opportunity to confirm the propriety of his decisions in Chicago and elsewhere during the strike and boycott. Nothing in his Supreme Court arguments suggested his new interest in arbitration of disputes between railroad capital and labor. Then, the day after the Supreme Court decided in *In re Debs* in exactly the way Olney had hoped, Secretary of State Walter Q. Gresham died, making available the very top spot in President Cleveland's cabinet. Olney followed his ambition. Within two weeks, he had been nominated by the president and confirmed by the Senate. Olney almost instantly shifted his attention from the domestic battle between capital and labor to foreign affairs.

If Olney looked back at all on the Pullman strike and legal proceedings, it may have been to savor the praise from the business and political communities for a job well done. "You are receiving much praise from every quarter for the firm and prompt action you have taken," Olney's brother Bill wrote to him. Too often "one fellow shakes the tree while the other fellow picks up and gets away with the persimmon." But in the present situation, Bill Olney added, the public understands "the great public service the Atty Genl. has rendered. . . . The public interest centers on the Pres. and his Atty Genl."

———

While Richard Olney softened his views and worked to reinforce his stature as a statesman following the Pullman case, Clarence Darrow in the aftermath of the proceedings became even more devoted to labor and developed his reputation as the nation's leading lawyer for the underdog. More so than the other major attorneys involved in the Pullman proceedings, Darrow began his work on the case while still a young man. As his tortured decision to leave the Chicago & Northwestern Railroad suggests, he was at the time of the case in the midst of figuring out what he stood for and, in a deep and personal way, who he was politically. The representation of Debs and the other union leaders dovetailed with Darrow's own quest, and as was true for Debs himself, the case can be said to have changed the course of an important public life.

In particular, Darrow realized through his representation of Debs and the others that he not only could argue for his labor clients but also could truly agree with their political and philosophical principles. Labor's views buoyed and inspired Darrow. Other lawyers had previously represented labor. Others had come forward in court to represent the interests of unions and their members. But in the past almost all of these attorneys had stood apart from their clients. Darrow, unwittingly at first but then with great conscious vigor, came genuinely to identify with his clients. His snipping attacks on Edwin Walker and Thomas Milchrist in the Chicago federal courts, it turned out, derived not from the litigator's delight in the game of courtroom combat but rather from a deep-seated resentment of the men who protected capital. Darrow's stirring rhetoric in both his appellate brief and his oral argument for the United States Supreme Court in *In re Debs*, it became clear, grew out of a commitment to righting the wrongs perpetrated against working men and women. If Darrow seemed particularly belligerent in the Pullman proceedings, it was because he came honestly to see himself as a warrior in a just crusade against exploiting, manipulating, hungry, and vindictive capital.

One result of Darrow's work in the Pullman case was his emergence as the leading labor lawyer of the early twentieth century. Time and again, individual labor leaders and unions called on him to represent their interests and overall cause. Darrow enjoyed the assignment and even reveled in it. Only gradually did labor realize that its confidence in Darrow had to be modulated. Although Darrow on more than one subsequent occasion represented labor in proceedings before the Supreme Court, this was not his greatest lawyerly strength. To be frank, he never became especially skillful at appellate argument. He was not adept at converting his passion and outrage into legal arguments that could persuade appellate judges. His real strength, it became evident as World War I approached, was in the trial courts, speaking to jurors rather than appellate judges. Jurors were the people most likely to moved by Darrow's rhetorical underscoring of the immense inequalities in the industrial sector.

{ *The Pullman Case* }

If this was a refinement of sorts in Darrow's calling, simultaneous expansions took place as well. Darrow's work in the Pullman case led him not only to side with labor but also to become a champion of other underdogs as well. As one of Darrow's many biographers has observed, "In time Darrow would come to regard almost any exercise of authority as pretentious, and to take particular delight in challenging its tribunes and pricking its balloons." Government, it seemed to Darrow, had fallen disastrously into the hands of private interest. Law and legal institutions were the handmaidens of power, and as a result they deserved no special respect. In keeping with his distaste of power clothed in law, Darrow opposed any exercise of authoritarian control. In the words of still another pair of Darrow biographers,

> Darrow's defense of Debs established him as a leading labor attorney on the national scene. . . . His reputation then burgeoned among the poor, the weak, the misunderstood. His office was filled with representatives of labor unions, political dissidents, relatives of men and women charged with criminal offenses from petty larceny to robbery to murder. All sought his help, and seldom were they turned away. . . . Almost half of the cases he took in his lifetime were without payment.

Overall, Darrow moved on from the Pullman case in positive and lasting ways. The practice of law is, for most, a relatively alienating experience. Lawyers tend in the course of their careers to put aside political beliefs and personal values in favor of a "neutral" approach to practice. That is, the client's goals become for the moment the lawyer's goals. When this happens often enough, the lawyer loses sight of whatever original goals he or she might have had. Darrow emerges as a countermodel to all this. Instead of developing a neutral private practice in which any cause was a good cause, he developed what might be cast as a "praxis," that is, a career of lawyer's work consistent with what had become his political position and philosophy. The Pullman case made Darrow into one lawyer in a thousand, and in subsequent decades many individuals and American society as a whole benefited.

Like Attorney General Olney, the trial and appellate court judges in the Pullman case heard some degree of insinuation that they were in the pockets of capital *and* even more praise for the fine and responsible work they had done. Judges get stroked, and most like it. Judges Peter S. Grosscup and William A. Woods continued to serve on the Chicago federal bench, although neither, contrary to Woods's fervent hopes, went on to bigger and better things. Justice David J. Brewer, meanwhile, continued his service on the United States Supreme Court until his death at the age of seventy-three in 1910.

In Grosscup's case developments related to his ties to railroads came back to haunt him. He served as a judge of the United States District Court until 1899, and from 1899 to 1908 he sat on the United States Court of Appeals. Then scandal struck. Charles H. Aldrich, a Chicago attorney who had earlier endorsed Grosscup for his federal judgeship, notified the United States attorney general that Grosscup was asking the railroads for free transportation for himself, for his family, and for others. Aldrich also alleged that Grosscup and his clerk were improperly involved with and enriched by other clients coming before the court in conjunction with railroad receiverships. In the wake of the allegations, Judge Grosscup resigned his judgeship.

Judge Woods, meanwhile, seemed inclined to keep rewriting the opinion on which he had worked so long and hard during the fall of 1894. Woods in April 1897 published a long essay in the *Yale Law Journal* concerning labor injunctions in the federal courts and, in essence, defending his own opinion regarding the Chicago injunction. "It is hard to believe that any one in his sober senses thinks the imprisonment of Debs a dangerous precedent," Woods said in the essay. Employing for a second time the denigration of the mental capacity of those who might disagree, Woods added,

> Nobody in his right mind believes that there has been usurpation of the power by the courts, or that the power exercised is the source or beginning of peril to individual or collective rights. Out of all that had been done by the courts since the Government was founded there can be deduced no sound reason for depriving them of their accustomed and well-understood power to enforce respect and order in their presence, and to compel obedience to their writs and commands wherever lawfully sent.

More interesting than the peccadilloes and self-serving apologetics of Judges Grosscup and Woods was the subsequent career of Justice David J. Brewer, who had spoken so eagerly for the unanimous United States Supreme Court in *In re Debs*. Brewer spent an additional fifteen years on the Supreme Court, and his formal judicial opinions did little to dispel notions that he was a friend of capital and a foe of labor. In a second 1895 decision growing out of the Pullman strike and boycott, Brewer vigorously upheld a conviction for labor conspiracy. He also ruled, in a number of cases, against workers seeking compensation for workplace injuries, even in one opinion proving more conservative that his uncle, Justice Stephen Field, thought by many in the period to be the single most conservative member of an overwhelmingly conservative Supreme Court.

Brewer also lectured widely in the early twentieth century, indeed too frequently for the tastes of some of his colleagues. His lectures did not blindly champion profit seeking, but they did assert that corporate wrongdoing was overestimated. The way to deal with it, to the extent it existed, was not trust busting but rather publicizing distasteful corporate practices—for example, blacklisting. In the area of capital-labor relations, Brewer evolved in ways comparable to Olney. Brewer did not oppose unionism, but he did defend the labor injunction as a way to "prevent wrong and violence." One of the more pronounced themes of his lectures was the need for obedience to the law. Echoing the final paragraphs of his *In re Debs* opinion, Brewer condemned lawbreakers, especially violence-prone strikers.

Oliver Wendell Holmes quoted President Theodore Roosevelt as saying Brewer had "a sweet-bread for a brain," but when Brewer collapsed and died after addressing a meeting of the Washington Literary Club on the subject of labor relations, most found a way to appreciate his accomplishments. Not surprisingly, the Pullman decision surfaced in many of the eulogies. The edges of the arguments and holding in the actual case had worn off by 1910, but eulogists recalled Brewer's commitment to the ballot box, the legislative process, and the courts. Brewer, in the words of Henry E. Davis, speaking to the Bar of the United States Supreme Court, was "the great civic apostle." Professor Edward S. Corwin said Brewer had been determined to restore the notion "of judges as moral mentors of the people."

—————

If United States Supreme Court justices and judges in general are "moral mentors" of the American people, what were their attitudes and what lessons did they teach in the Pullman case? The law, after all, operated primarily through the courts in the whole controversy. Little was heard from legislatures, and with the exception of the Justice Department, the executive branch was more concerned with when and how to use federal troops. What did the judges and the courts have to say about capital and labor?

What legal prescriptions and proscriptions did they offer regarding the relations of capital and labor? What were their messages for industrial America, and what importance did these messages have in subsequent years?

The case on the most obvious level illustrated that labor could expect to find few friends on the federal bench. A few judges—Judge Peter S. Grosscup springs to mind as a possible example—might quite literally have been in the pockets of capital; they might have been on the monetary take. But more generally, the men who came to serve on the bench in turn-of-the-century America had backgrounds and worldviews more comparable to those of capital than to those of labor. When disputes between capital and labor came before them, they were much more likely to accept capital's arguments. In a majority of the cases, the acceptance of these arguments was neither corrupt nor disingenuous. The judges simply heard the arguments as more persuasive.

However, the reactions to these arguments could in addition be quite intemperate and even vindictive. One legal historian has underscored how judges in Debs's era and later frequently portrayed labor activists and strikers as foreign, shiftless, irrational, and, most notably, prone to violence. Another legal historian has commented on the same phenomenon and coined the term "semi-outlawry." Judges in industrial America were inclined to see strikers as hooligans, outlaws, lawbreakers, and criminals.

All of this was evident in the Pullman case. In the Chicago proceedings the judges heard of and were influenced by the single telegram from Debs that even hinted at violence. It seemed the classic smoking gun because it confirmed what the judges wanted to think about labor activists in the first place. In his lengthy opinion upholding the contempt citation, Judge William A. Woods talked of a violent conspiracy and, in particular, of men undermining bridges and thereby sending people to their deaths. The strike and boycott leaders, Woods had said, were responsible "for giving up a city to disorder and paralyzing the industries and commerce of the country."

Even on the United States Supreme Court level, Justice David Brewer in his opinion in *In re Debs* continued, consciously or unconsciously, to couple the strikers with images of lawbreaking, disorder, and violence. At several points he underscored the conduct of a "mob" and the problem of "mob violence." Even the most genuinely aggrieved worker, Brewer said, had no warrant "to invite as a means of redress the cooperation of a mob, with its accompanying acts of violence." Puffing his masculine chest, Brewer warned that "the strong arm of government" could and should "brush away" both the problems caused by the lawless strikers and, if need be, the lawless strikers themselves. All of these statements, in the parlance of legal education, are "dicta," that is, nonessential commentary in conjunction with the precise holding of a case. Yet dicta often suggest just what drives their judicial authors. They reveal to us policy preferences, political alignments, and raw bias.

Eugene Debs, whose sometimes confused involvement in the Pullman case might be thought of as his "legal education," was ultimately not oblivious to what had transpired. When he later composed his famous, and for some inspiring, conversion-to-socialism essay, the judicial impression that he, leaders of the American Railway Union, and labor activists in general were lawless criminals grated on him. In fact, he made an effort in the essay to turn the tables—to deplore the lawlessness of the legal system and its champions. He spoke forcefully in the essay of how the "lawful" authorities in the midst of the Pullman strike sacked and destroyed the American Railway Union offices, of how men he considered lawbreakers harassed and abused strikers, and of how a failure to tell the true criminals from the purported ones reigned. The implication, of course, was that the judges and the legal system in general had gotten things wrong. Later, during his long, dogged career as a socialist political spokesman, Debs often engaged in a comparable attempt to reverse the negative referencing, to reverse the characterizing of the legitimate and the illegitimate.

The most important legal issue in the Pullman case involved the labor injunction. Prompted by the "bill in equity" filed by Edwin Walker and Thomas Milchrist on July 2, 1894, and issued by Judges Grosscup and Woods on the same day, the injunction was the crucial legal order in the case. If extracted from history and invited to stand on its own, the injunction and especially its omnibus features might rankle many modern critics. In the period, meanwhile, reactions were for the most part different. Most Americans thought strikes and boycotts, and certainly something like the Pullman strike and boycott, should be stopped. Railroad traffic in most of the country stalled or stopped. Even the United States mails could not get through. Surely the courts should be able to do something about this, and the issuance and enforcement of an injunction were viable steps that could be taken.

The labor injunction in the Pullman case was not the first of its kind. Debs himself had, at least from a distance, observed the workings of another one in the 1888 strike against the Chicago, Burlington and Quincy Railroad, which had nudged him on his way toward industrial unionism. Through the late 1880s and into the 1890s capital refined the tool for the suppression of strikes and boycotts. As noted, it was replacing the conspiracy prosecution as a legal device to control uncooperative workers. Scholars in the 1940s estimated that between 1880 and 1930, as many as eighteen hundred injunctions were issued against labor strikes and boycotts. A more recent scholar has upped the count, saying a better estimate for the same period is forty-three hundred.

In this forest of injunctions the Pullman injunction stood tallest. The Pullman strike and boycott were of unprecedented magnitude, and the American population followed developments with fear and concern. In addition, the case wended its way to the United States Supreme Court, and *In re Debs* was the first time the nation's highest tribunal ruled in favor of a labor injunction. The injunction in the Pullman case and the Supreme Court's ultimate endorsement of both the injunction itself and a contempt citation for violating it were exceptionally important and influential embodiments of capital's attempt to use injunctions against labor. The case is the hinge on which this legalistic intervention in capital/labor relations swings.

Labor injunctions remained a powerful weapon for capital until precluded by the Norris–La Guardia Act of 1932, and it is revealing that this change came not from the federal courts but rather from a Congress and an executive influenced by Depression Era concerns. The federal trial and appellate courts, with their hostile attitudes regarding labor and their acceptance of labor injunctions, had been "mentors" of a special sort. They thought labor should stay in its place, and they were prepared to use injunctions to make that happen when called upon to do so.

By the time of the Norris–La Guardia Act, unions themselves had taken a more conservative turn. Broad-based political programs and a class analysis drained out of the labor movement. Union members ceased to speak of the struggle between "capital" and "labor" and focused instead on goals such as job security, higher wages, improved working conditions, and collective bargaining. According to one historian, "Union politics ceased to be the diffuse politics of a popular movement and became instead the tightly-focused lobbying strategies of an economic interest group."

Scholars have characterized this turn in the American labor movement in various ways. For some, it is a matter of "voluntarism," that is, a commitment to attaining better working conditions and raising wages through negotiations and contracts. It would be too simple to understand this voluntarism as dating from the beginning of the Republic, but labor did even before the Norris–La Guardia Act begin settling for collective bargaining rather than political debate. Other scholars have spoken of labor's new "prudential unionism," that is, a studied cautiousness in the workplace and certain withdrawal from more radical political positions. For still others, the turn is toward not "prudential" but rather "business" unionism. Unions, it seemed increasingly, were devoted to self-interested economic goals rather than broader political goals.

None of these characterizations discount the important wage-and-hour legislation achieved by labor in the 1930s and later. Unions did in fact get themselves to the economic bargaining table. Many union members did get themselves to the suburbs and their children into college. But labor, the labor movement, and almost all unions in the process of these achievements assumed places as participants rather than sharp critics of advanced capitalism. Wage labor was accepted as a system, and many workers took the American dream to be not economic independence but rather an elevated level of consumption.

The role of the courts, law, and especially the labor injunction should not be underestimated as a factor in this much-discussed conservative evolution of American labor. One need not lapse into the presumption prevalent in law school corridors that the world revolves around law to appreciate law as a major factor in the "taming" of the American labor movement. The courts' sanctioning of the labor injunction backed up by the muscle of the army not only ended the Pullman strike and boycott but also made it the last large-scale labor insurrection. Never again would American labor imagine something approaching a general strike. The courts' often hostile and menacing antistrike and antiboycott decrees scared unions into compliance and helped send them down the voluntarist, prudent, and businesslike road. Law in the Pullman case and in general did not single-handedly create accommodating and conservative unionism in industrial America, but it certainly contributed to that development.

———

In conclusion, the complex Pullman case also offers suggestions about the very nature of law in battles between capital and labor in the context of industrial America. Law—understood as a set of institutions and also a complex of prescriptions and proscriptions—was hardly a neutral force standing above social life and regulating it in fair and balanced ways. Images of prosecutors working simultaneously for the government and for the railroads and of judges helping those prosecutors shape their petitions before submitting them preclude any comfortable acceptance of the standard American ideological belief in a rule of law. But at the same time, law does not seem simply a tool available whenever needed by the railroads and by capital in general. The criminal prosecution of Debs and the other American Railway Union leaders—something the railroads wanted badly—went awry. Indeed, once the United States Supreme Court ruled in *In re Debs,* Olney instructed Walker to forego remounting the criminal prosecution that had been terminated because of a sick juror. The defendants never were reprosecuted, let alone convicted. At the Supreme Court level, the justices' upholding of the contempt citation may have been virtually certain, but still, the justices wrestled with the arguments and precedents and were not disingenuous in their conclusions.

Law emerges from the entire controversy as a fluid, contested, contradicted discourse grounded in history and power. In the era, capital had greater power than labor. The lawmakers and judges for the most part understood law the way capital did; even more profoundly, the lawmakers and judges also understood the world in ways capital did. But times and power differentials change. In a later period the Congress and courts were receptive to a more moderate labor movement's preferences. Springing from the lesson about law's social identity in the Pullman case, modern law reformers should be better able to make their way in the fluid, contested, contradicted legal discourse of their own era.

March 3, 1831	George Pullman, the third child and third son of James Lewis and Emily Caroline Minton Pullman, is born not far from Buffalo, New York.
November 5, 1855	Eugene Debs, the fourth child and first son of Jean Daniel and Marguerite Marie Bettrich Debs, is born in Terre Haute, Indiana.
January 1859	George Pullman launches a Chicago business devoted to raising downtown buildings from the city's mud.
February 22, 1867	The Illinois legislature grants to George Pullman a corporate charter for the Pullman Palace Car Company.
January 1, 1881	George Pullman opens his new company town of "Pullman" to the south of Chicago on a previously unincorporated tract near Lake Calumet. All housing and other facilities are owned by the company.
June 20, 1893	Eugene Debs and others meet in Chicago and found the American Railway Union, a labor organization open to all Caucasian workers (with the exception of managerial employees) who are employed by railroads.
Spring 1894	The American Railway Union prevails in a strike against the Great Northern Railroad, leading to greatly expanded membership for the union.
May 11, 1894	Workers, some of whom are members of the American Railway Union, strike the car works of the Pullman Palace Car Company, located in the town of Pullman.
June 26, 1894	Members of the American Railway Union begin refusing to move or handle any Pullman cars, in solidarity with striking workers at the Pullman plant.
July 2, 1894	Chicago federal judges Peter S. Grosscup and William A. Woods issue an injunction ordering American Railway Union officers to stop interfering with rail traffic and to allow passage of the United States mail.
July 4, 1894	Acting on the order of President Grover Cleveland, federal troops under the command of General Nelson A. Miles enter Chicago to quell rioting, free blockaded trains, and allow the delivery of the United States mail.

July 6, 1894	In the worst single day of rioting, Chicago mobs destroy over seven hundred railroad cars and other railroad property.
July 17, 1894	With Chicago rioting and protests under control, federal troops are ordered to leave Chicago, and workers begin returning to their jobs at the Pullman Palace Car Company.
December 14, 1894	United States Circuit Court Judge William A. Woods rules that Eugene Debs and others were in contempt of court for violating the injunction issued on July 2, 1894. The defendants are ordered to serve sentences of three to six months in the McHenry County Jail in Woodstock, Illinois.
March 25–26, 1895	Lyman Trumbull, Stephen Gregory, and Clarence Darrow argue against Edward Whitney, Edwin Walker, and Richard Olney before the United States Supreme Court in oral arguments concerning the Debs contempt citation.
May 27, 1895	A unanimous United States Supreme Court speaking through Justice David J. Brewer upholds the contempt citation of Eugene Debs and others in *In re Debs.*
June 11, 1895	All of the defendants except for Eugene Debs report to the jail in Woodstock, Illinois, to begin serving their sentences for contempt. Debs himself arrives one day late, citing a meal with bad cucumbers.
January 1, 1897	Eugene Debs announces that he has become a socialist.
October 19, 1897	George Pullman dies in Chicago.
October 20, 1926	Eugene Debs dies in the Lindlahr Sanitarium in northern Illinois.

{ *The Pullman Case* }

BIBLIOGRAPHICAL ESSAY

Note from the Series Editors: The following bibliographical essay contains the major primary and secondary sources the author consulted for this volume. We have asked all authors in the series to omit formal citations in order to make our volumes more readable, inexpensive, and appealing for students and general readers. In adopting this format, Landmark Law Cases and American Society follows the precedent of a number of highly regarded and widely consulted series.

Most of the important primary materials regarding the Pullman case are in Chicago. The National Archives–Great Lakes Division has the original trial court records for the case, most of them handwritten in large ledger books. Other primary materials relating to the case are in the Chicago Historical Society, The Newberry Library, and the Chicago Public Library. The latter's Harold Washington Library Center houses a particularly useful microfilm collection of Chicago daily newspapers from the 1890s. A wealth of information and interviews with strike participants are available in the United States Strike Commission's *Report on the Chicago Strike of June–July, 1894* (Washington, D.C.: Government Printing Office, 1895).

Secondary works on Chicago are abundant. The classic study is Bessie Louise Pierce's multivolume work. Her third volume, *A History of Chicago: The Rise of a Modern City, 1871–93* (New York: Alfred A. Knopf, 1957), nicely chronicles Chicago's dramatic late-nineteenth-century growth. More recent specialized studies include William Cronon's *Nature's Metropolis: Chicago and the Great West* (New York: W. W. Norton, 1991); Robin Einhorn's *Property Rules: Political Economy in Chicago, 1833–1872* (Chicago: University of Chicago Press, 1991); and Donald L. Miller's *City of the Century: The Epic of Chicago and the Making of America* (New York: Simon & Schuster, 1996). Treatments of Chicago history relating even more specifically to the Pullman controversy are James Gilbert's *Perfect Cities: Chicago's Utopias of 1893* (Chicago: University of Chicago Press, 1991) and Carl Smith's especially intriguing *Urban Disorder and the Shape of Belief: The Great Chicago Fire, the Haymarket Bomb, and the Model Town of Pullman* (Chicago: University of Chicago Press, 1995). An interesting and lively local history from the period right before the Pullman controversy is A. T. Andreas's *History of Chicago: From the Fire of 1871, Until 1885* (Chicago: A. T. Andreas Company, 1886).

Liston Edgington Leyendecker's *Palace Car Prince: A Biography of George Mortimer Pullman* (Boulder: University Press of Colorado, 1992) is a solid modern biography of the man who symbolized capital throughout the Pullman case. Stanley Buder's *Pullman: An Experiment in Industrial Order and Community Planning, 1880–1930* (New York: Oxford University Press, 1967) is a thoughtful study of the model town

Pullman developed along the banks of Lake Calumet. A useful sketch of the town of Pullman written just before the strike began is Mrs. Duane Doty's *The Town of Pullman* (1893; rpt. Chicago: Pullman Civic Organization, 1974). Primary materials involving George Pullman and Pullman Palace Car Company scrapbooks, patents, board minute books, and assorted memorabilia are available at the Chicago Historical Society and The Newberry Library.

Pullman, of course, is only one of a number of big business tycoons, and his story is only one part of the rise of big business in late-nineteenth-century America. A classic but still readable work on the great business figures of the era is Matthew Josephson's *The Robber Barons: The Great American Capitalists, 1861–1901* (New York: Harcourt, Brace, 1934). Alfred D. Chandler Jr. has been the leading historian regarding not business in general but rather the corporation, and his works include *Strategy and Structure: Chapters in the History of Industrial America* (Cambridge: M.I.T. Press, 1962); *The Visible Hand: The Management Revolution in American Business* (Cambridge: Belknap Press, 1977); and *Scale and Scope: The Dynamics of Industrial Capitalism* (Cambridge: Belknap Press, 1990). Alan Trachtenberg's *The Incorporation of America: Culture and Society in the Gilded Age* (New York: Hill and Wang, 1982) discusses the corporate system's impact on American culture.

Alfred D. Chandler has also edited a collection concerned with the railroad business, *The Railroads, The Nation's First Big Business: Sources and Readings* (New York: Harcourt, Brace and World, 1965). Other useful works focusing on just the railroads are Robert W. Fogel, *Railroads and Economic Growth: Essays in Econometric History* (Baltimore: Johns Hopkins University Press, 1964), and George R. Taylor and Irene Neu, *The American Railroad Network, 1861–1890* (Cambridge: Harvard University Press, 1956).

The free-labor ideology that was so powerful for Pullman and certain other leading businessmen of the era is captured well in Eric Foner's *Free Soil, Free Labor, Free Men: The Ideology of the Republican Party Before the Civil War* (1970; rpt. with new introductory essay, New York: Oxford University Press, 1995). Other fine works exploring free-labor ideology are Robert J. Steinfeld's *The Invention of Free Labor: The Employment Relation in English and American Law and Culture, 1350–1870* (Chapel Hill: University of North Carolina Press, 1991) and Jonathan A. Glickstein, *Concepts of Free Labor in Antebellum America* (New Haven: Yale University Press, 1991).

Works that address at least in part the relationships of capital, corporations, and the law include Tony Freyer's *Regulating Big Business: Antitrust in Great Britain and America, 1880–1990* (New York: Cambridge University Press, 1992) and Herbert Hovenkamp's *Enterprise and American Law, 1836–1937* (Cambridge: Harvard University Press, 1991). A more specialized work exploring the relationship of the 1893 depression to the merger movement is Naomi R. Lamoreaux's *The Great Merger Movement in American Business, 1895–1904* (New York: Cambridge University Press, 1985). Gabriel Kolko's *Railroads and Regulation 1877–1916* (Princeton: Princeton University Press, 1965) explores government efforts to control, direct, and enhance railroad growth. Gerald G. Eggert's *Railroad Labor Disputes: The Beginnings of Federal Strike Policy* (Ann Arbor: University of Michigan Press, 1967) comments extensively on the impact of the Pullman strike.

Eugene Debs has been graced with excellent biographies in two different eras. Ray Ginger's *The Bending Cross: A Biography of Eugene Victor Debs* (New Brunswick: Rutgers University Press, 1949) is written with great thoroughness, admiration, and passion. Nick Salvatore's even longer *Eugene V. Debs: Citizen and Socialist* (Urbana: University of Illinois Press, 1982) acknowledges more of Debs's failings but nevertheless offers a persuasive interpretation of Debs as an indigenous American radical in the republican tradition. Another useful and engaging study of Debs is Harold W. Currie's *Eugene V. Debs* (Boston: Twayne Publishers, 1976); the volume synthesizes Debs's thoughts in various subject areas. H. Wayne Morgan's *Eugene V. Debs: Socialist for President* (New York: New York University Press, 1962) treats Debs's political career in the decades after the Pullman case. My own synthesis of Debs's legal thought is "Eugene Debs as Legal Heretic: The Law-Related Conversion, Catechism and Evangelism of an American Socialist," *University of Cincinnati Law Review* 63, no. 1 (1994): 339–75.

Debs's only full-length book is *Walls and Bars* (1927; rpt., Monclair, N.J.: Patterson Smith, 1973), a collection of essays on prison conditions that Debs wrote along with socialist journalist David Karsner thirty years after the Pullman case. A useful collection of Debs's most important speeches and editorial writings, complete with an introduction by Arthur M. Schlesinger Jr., is *Writings and Speeches of Eugene V. Debs* (New York: Hermitage Press, 1949). Another useful collection is Jean Y. Tussey, ed., *Eugene V. Debs Speaks* (New York: Pathfinder Press, 1970). Individual items in these collections that are especially intriguing for purposes of the volume at hand are "Liberty" (a speech given in Chicago after his 1895 release from jail), "The Role of the Courts" (a speech given in Terre Haute after completion of the term in Woodstock), and "How I Became a Socialist" (a short article published in 1897).

The best repositories of primary materials involving Eugene Debs are in Terre Haute, Indiana. The Cunningham Library at Indiana State University has almost five thousand letters to and from Debs. The Debs Foundation also has a large collection of letters, as well as other memorabilia. The foundation superbly maintains Debs's adult home, the home to which he returned time and again after labor actions and political campaigns. The second floor of the home is used as a Debs museum. For those unable to journey to Terre Haute, J. Robert Constantine's *Letters of Eugene V. Debs*, 3 vols. (Urbana: University of Illinois Press, 1990) affords a way to explore Debs's private thoughts and remarkably wide circle of friends both inside and outside the labor movement.

The scholarly literature on American labor of course stretches far beyond Debs, the American Railway Union, and the Socialist Party, including as it does histories of both American labor organizations and the American working experience. Of special interest in the context of the work at hand are historical studies relating to labor and law. These include Christopher Tomlins's fine work regarding law and labor in the first half of the nineteenth century, *Law, Labor and Ideology in the Early American Republic* (New York: Cambridge University Press, 1993). For the second half of the nineteenth century and continuing into the early twentieth century, important scholarly works include William Forbath's *Law and the Shaping of the American Labor Movement* (Cambridge: Harvard University Press, 1991); Victoria Hattam's *Labor Visions and State Power: The Origins of Business Unionism in the United States* (Princeton: Princeton University Press, 1993); Karen Orren's *Belated Feudalism: Labor, the Law, and Liberal Development in the United States* (New York: Cambridge University Press, 1991); and Christopher Tomlins's *The State and the Unions: Labor Relations, Law and the Organized Labor Movement in America, 1880–1960* (New York: Cambridge University Press, 1985). William G. Ross's *A Muted Fury: Populists, Progressives and Labor Unions Confront the Courts, 1890–1937* (Princeton: Princeton University Press, 1993) compares the success of the labor unions in the American courts to that of other self-styled progressives.

The most accomplished and thorough work on the Pullman strike is Almont Lindsey's *The Pullman Strike: The Story of a Unique Experiment and of a Great Labor Upheaval* (Chicago: University of Chicago Press, 1942). Although over a half century old, the work remains insightful and provocative. A useful collection of documents and materials relating to the strike is Colston E. Warne's *The Pullman Boycott of 1894: The Problem of Federal Intervention* (Boston: D.C. Heath and Company, 1955). Larry Peterson's "The Changing Image of Labor Conflict in the 1890s: Corporate, Labor, Government, and Media Attempts to Mold Public Perceptions of the Pullman Strike" is one of several fine essays in *The Pullman Strike and the Crisis of the State* (Urbana: University of Illinois Press, 1998), a collection edited by Richard Schneirov, Nick Salvatore, and Shelton Stromquist in commemoration of the one-hundredth anniversary of the strike. Useful contemporary accounts of the strike include W. Burns's *The Pullman Boycott, A Complete History of the Great R.R. Strike* (St. Paul: McGill Printing Company, 1894) and especially the Reverend William Carwardine's *The Pullman Strike* (1894; rpt. Chicago: Illinois Labor History Society, 1973). Carwardine was a minister based in the very town of Pullman.

A number of the lawyers and judges who toiled in the Pullman case have themselves been the subjects of biographies or have written their own autobiographies. A fine early biography of Richard Olney is Henry James's *Richard Olney and His Public Service* (Boston: Houghton Mifflin Company, 1923). A more recent and equally distinguished work is Gerald G. Eggert's *Richard Olney—Evolution of a Statesman* (University Park: Pennsylvania State University Press, 1974).

Studies of Clarence Darrow begin with Irving Stone's famous but overwritten *Clarence Darrow for the Defense* (New York: Doubleday, Doran and Company, 1941). More recent and well executed biographies are Kevin Tierney's *Darrow—A Biography* (New York: Thomas Y. Crowell, 1979) and Arthur and Lila Weinberg's

Clarence Darrow: A Sentimental Rebel (New York: G. P. Putnam's Sons, 1980). A lengthy bibliography of works by and about Darrow is Willard D. Hunsberger, *Clarence Darrow, A Bibliography* (Matuchin, N.J.: Scarecrow Press, 1981). Darrow's own autobiography is *The Story of My Life* (New York: C. Scribner's Sons, 1934).

Works on Lyman Trumbull, the senior lawyer and former United States senator who joined Debs's defense team for purposes of the appeal to the United States Supreme Court, include Horace White's early *The Life of Lyman Trumbull* (Boston: Houghton Mifflin Company, 1913). More recent works are Mark M. Krug's *Lyman Trumbull: Conservative Radical* (New York: A. S. Barnes and Company, 1965) and Ralph J. Roske's *His Own Counsel: The Life and Times of Lyman Trumbull* (Reno: University of Nevada Press, 1979).

The life of Justice John Marshall Harlan, who brought the Debs case to the full United States Supreme Court, is discussed in Tinsley E. Yarbrough's *Judicial Enigma: The First Justice Harlan* (New York: Oxford University Press, 1995). A good recent biography of the Supreme Court justice who wrote the *In re Debs* opinion is David J. Brodhead's *David J. Brewer: The Life of a Supreme Court Justice, 1837–1910* (Carbondale: Southern Illinois Press, 1994). An older study that mentions individual justices as well as many others in law is Arnold M. Paul's *Conservative Crisis and the Rule of Law: Attitudes of Bench and Bar, 1887–1895* (Ithaca: Cornell University Press, 1960).

As for the entire subject of industrial America, Walter Licht's *Industrializing America—The Nineteenth Century* (Baltimore: The Johns Hopkins University Press, 1995) is a compact and especially useful study. Other works that attempt in a sense to address the whole socioeconomic context of the Pullman case include Thomas C. Cochran and William Miller's early *The Age of Enterprise: A Social History of Industrial America* (New York: Macmillan Company, 1942) and, more recently, Robert Higgs's *The Transformation of the American Economy, 1865–1914: An Essay in Interpretation* (New York: Wiley, 1971), Brooke Hindle and Steven Lubar's *Engines of Change: The American Industrial Revolution, 1780–1860* (Washington, D.C.: Smithsonian Institution Press, 1986), and Bruce Laurie's *Artisans into Workers: Labor in Nineteenth-Century America* (New York: Hill and Wang, 1989).

INDEX